POLI

BOOKS OF RELATED INTEREST

The New Mediterranean Democracies: Regime Transition in Greece, Spain and Portugal
edited by Geoffrey Pridham

Israel, Turkey and Greece: Uneasy Relations in the East Mediterranean
by Amikam Nachmani

Jews, Christians, and Muslims in the Mediterranean World after 1492
edited by Alisa Meyuhas Ginio
(new in paperback)

Intercultural Contacts in the Medieval Mediterranean
edited by Benjamin Arbel

Latins and Greeks in the Eastern Mediterranean after 1204
edited by Benjamin Arbel, Bernard Hamilton and David Jacoby

Spain and the Mediterranean since 1898
edited by Raanan Rein

Seafaring and the Jews
Edited by Nadav Kashtan

POLITICAL USES OF THE PAST

The Recent Mediterranean Experience

Editors

JACQUES REVEL

GIOVANNI LEVI

FRANK CASS

LONDON • PORTLAND OR

First published in 2002 in Great Britain by
FRANK CASS AND COMPANY LIMITED
Crown House, 47 Chase Side, Southgate, London N14 BP, England

and in the United States of America by
FRANK CASS
c/o International Specialized Book Services, Inc.
5824 N.E. Hassalo Street, Portland, Oregon 927213-3640

British Library Cataloguing in Publication Data

Political uses of the past : the recent Mediterranean
experience
1. History – Political aspects – Mediterranean Region
2. Group identity – Mediterranean Region – History –
20th century 3. Mediterranean Region – Historiography
I. Revel, Jaques, 1942– II. Levi, Giovanni, 1939–
909′.09822

ISBN 0 7146 5271 7 (h/back)
ISBN 0 7146 8244 6 (p/back)

Library of Congress Cataloging-in-Publication Data

The recent Mediterranean experience / editors, Jaques Revel, Giovanni
Levi.
p. cm.
ISBN 0-7146-5271-7 (cloth) – ISBN 0-7146-8244-6 (pbk.)
1. Mediterranean Region–Ethnic relations. 2. Mediterranean
Region–Historiography. 3. Mediterranean Region–Politics and
government. 4. Religion and politics–Mediterranean Region. 5.
Europe–Politics and government–20th century. 6. Human
geography–Mediterranean Region. I. Revel, Jaques, 1942– II. Levi,
Giovanni, 1939–.
D973 .R43 2001
909′.098222–dc

This group of studies first appeared in a Special Issue of *Mediterranean Historical Review* (ISSN 0951-8967), Vol.16, No.1 (June 2001), [Political Uses of the Past: The Recent Mediterranean Experience].

Printed in Great Britain by Antony Rowe Ltd., Chippenham, Wiltshire

Contents

Preface	*Irad Malkin*	vii
Historians and the Present Conjuncture	*François Hartog and Jacques Revel*	1
Towards an Ethnographic Phenomenology of the Greek Spirit	*Michael Herzfeld*	13
The Construction of National Time: The Making of the Modern Greek Historical Imagination	*Antonis Liakos*	27
Shifting Boundaries, Clientalism and Balkan Identities	*Drago Roksandič*	43
Notes on Two Discordant Histories: Armenia during World War I	*Lucette Valensi*	49
The Distant Past: On the Political Use of History	*Giovanni Levi*	61
The Two Levels of Public Use of the Past	*Claudio Pavone*	74
Out of Place, Out of Time	*Elias Sanbar*	87
Political Uses of History in Spain	*Pedro-Ruiz Torres*	95
Abstracts		117
List of Contributors		120
Index		122

Preface

This publication is the result of cooperation between the Center for Mediterranean Civilizations at Tel Aviv University together with its academic journal the *Mediterranean Historical Review* and a group of scholars associated with the Centro di Studi Mediterranei. It follows an international conference organized by Jacques Revel and Giovanni Levi on 'The Political Uses of the Past' organized by the Centro di Studi Mediterranei at the Istituto Italiano per gli Studi Flosofici of Naples, on 29–30 January 1999. I would like to take this opportunity to thank all the participants, the guest editors, Anthony Molho, moving spirit behind the Centro di Studi Mediterranei, Francesca Trivellato of Venice for her enormous help in the organization of the conference, and especially Avvocato Gerardo Marotta, President of the Istituto Italiano per gli Studi Flosofici, whose help and support have been generous and warm. Special thanks are also due to Ilit Ferber, managing editor of the *Mediterranean Historical Review*, for coordinating translations, proof-reading and producing this volume.

For the past three millennia the Mediterranean has functioned as a vast network and infrastructure for its civilizations, oscillating between unitary and diversionary forces and perceptions. Its images have come to play varying roles along with changing historical contexts. Mussolini's revival of the Roman *mare nostrum* (or rather, the Fascist representation of Roman ideas associated with the Mediterranean) may serve as a convenient illustration for a neo-unitary, political use of the ancient Mediterranean past in recent history. However, today the Mediterranean knows no single, national or imperial ideology. By its very nature, current Mediterranean discourse emphasizes the multifarious nature of its contacts; 'network', rather than face-to-face nations, have become its byword. And yet the historical uses of the past in the recent Mediterranean experience often sound (anachronistically?) national or ethnic. This is evident not only in contacts among Mediterranean countries and societies, but especially in the construction of the collective identity of each.

Jacques Revel and François Hartog provide us with an essay that also serves as an introduction to the entire volume, followed by the individual contributions. This volume does not pretend to cover all Mediterranean countries, but to examine some prominent and potentially comparable issues. Some papers from the conference, covering topics such as modern colonization in north Africa and contemporary historiography in Israel, failed to reach us in time for publication. With regard to the current situation in the Middle East, Elias Sanbar asked to withdraw his paper however, since the volume was already in production, this was impossible.

The *Mediterranean Historical Review* that hosts this publication has been active since 1986, studying comparative and comparable phenomena of Mediterranean history. Having matured in years and reputation, it now turns to a double-reflective question: historians discussing the uses of history especially when such uses, in and of themselves, stimulate or even produce new kinds of collective representations that are directly effective in history. Its editors, Alisa Meyuhas Ginio and Irad Malkin, are happy to offer this collection of essays and are grateful to both Jacques Revel and Giovanni Levi for conceptualizing and editing this work.

Irad Malkin
Director
Center for Mediterranean Civilizations
Editor
Mediterranean Historical Review
Tel Aviv University

Historians and the Present Conjuncture

FRANÇOIS HARTOG and JACQUES REVEL

The political uses of the past have been a classic, even a common, theme in the reflections of historians ever since they first took up this paradoxical activity of producing a true discourse about what time conceals from human observation. Professional historians are not the only users of the past – far from it: not only powers or authorities and institutions but also individuals are constantly tempted to mobilize the cognitive, argumentative, and symbolic resources of the past. Historians have long been aware of this temptation. When they became a professional community in the second half of the nineteenth century, the problem of objectivity – 'that noble dream' – was at the heart of the debate about identity which brought them together.[1] They knew full well that they had to guard against the fascination of politics, and they believed that they had found the means of doing so partly by adopting the precepts of positivism but mainly by keeping their objects at a distance. This was clearly stated in the introduction to the very first issue of the *Revue Historique* (1876), which tends to be considered something akin to a birth certificate of the discipline in France. Addressing future contributors, the article recommended 'avoiding contemporary controversies, addressing the subjects of their studies with the methodological rigor and absence of bias required by science, and not seeking arguments for or against any theories involved indirectly only'. Gabriel Monod then explained the insufficient progress of the discipline as resulting from 'political and religious passions' which, in 'the absence of a scientific tradition', had not been curbed. Hence the utmost restraint was called for.

A quarter of a century later it was obvious that these wise warnings had not stood the test of time. And yet, did not the scholarly skills of the positive method play a decisive role in the expert reports given in the Dreyfus affair? And were not those armed with them capable of distinguishing the true from the false under all circumstances? Nevertheless, a whiff of suspicion clung to overcontemporary history, which for a long time was a sensitive point. With the recent reserval in this tendency, it was then certainties of positive history which became suspect: were not the greatest scholars likely to continue confronting each other over the significance of the end of the

Roman Empire, the Investiture controversy, the Wars of Religion, or the absolute monarchy with the same ideological involvement as over the French Revolution or church–state relations in the nineteenth century? And so the illusion of evaluating everything coolly had to be abandoned.

Actually, any historical discourse is liable to political uses, whether through the intermediary of its author or its audience or because of the special relationship existing between them. Such is the case of narratives of origins establishing a particular human group's right to some particular tract of land, staking a claim to native roots there, or asserting the destiny of a nation by demonstrating its enduring continuity (such as the Gallic or Trojan origins long claimed by the French monarchy); narratives of founding or refounding, presenting an absolute beginning in such different ways as the American Revolution and the French Revolution; narratives of legitimation such as those which enabled Italian Fascism to invoke the Roman *Mare nostrum* to justify its imperial ambitions and allowed French colonization in North Africa to stake claims to the distant *pax romana*, citing archaeological finds as evidence; or, lastly, apologetics or gaps such as those which for a long time made it possible to forget difficult moments in the past such as Vichy or the Algerian War. It goes without saying that these variants criss-cross each other, mingling within historical discourses infinitely more complex and subtle than this elementary overview would suggest.

Some genres have mobilized these uses more than others, and they provide us with the most striking examples. National history is one such *par excellence*. Although this is perfectly predictable, it should be carefully examined for two reasons. The first is that it cannot be separated from the national experience which it is responsible for presenting as both natural and obvious. The second is that this biographical commentary on the nation must come to terms with tempos, periods, and modes which are both constraints and resources. The history of France is a canonical genre which, for centuries, had the role of guaranteeing the continuity of the nation for as long as possible and in a quasi-biological mode, establishing a community of destinies and demonstrating the special nature of the destiny of France.[2] The objection will be advanced that this is a singular experience because of its exceptional length and the tendency of the historians who have produced its narrative to overstress its continuity – for example, by inventing the biological continuity of the three royal bloodlines or by projecting a retrospective horoscope onto French territory, citing Caesar and Strabo to support it. But it is precisely on this point that national history must be of interest to us. What narrative construction is required to describe briefer collective experiences or an uncertain path, its continuity interrupted, hesitating between several options or even seeking proof on which to ground its legitimacy or disputing its proof with other users? Michael Herzfeld here reminds us of the tension which runs through Greek national construction from the nineteenth century on, in which a model of the universal Greek invented by German philologists and imported by the Bavarian monarchy with the help of Westernized elites confronts a regional, Oriental model combining Byzantine, Slav, Turkish, and Arab attributes. Where these two models clashed, there emerged a politics of memory but also of daily life – and, to tell the truth, politics *tout court*. This is the same Greek experience that is addressed, following a different process, by Antonis Liakos in reflecting on the construction of national narratives which help the players of the present (in this case, political players) to grasp the past – which suggests thinking about how people identify what suits them but also what is possible given the resources offered by this past and the constraints which, nevertheless, it imposes. This touches upon an entire set of questions which arise in connection with the national whole. Thus Elias Sanbar discusses the difficulty of making a historical discourse possible even where the need for one is considered urgent, as in the case of the Palestinians in Israel. This is an old problem, the same one that had to be resolved by the historians of the 1820 generation in France, who had to invent the means of reestablishing some sort of continuity, at least a transition, to bridge the radical break which the Revolution had created in the country's national destiny.[3] Such veering in historiography often involves long-term processes, but its own timeline may be far shorter. Pedro Ruiz Torres provides an enlightening demonstration of this by analyzing contemporary changes in the major conflicting readings of Spanish history.

Historians are in the front line of these large-scale manoeuvres because they produce the more or less authorized versions of the past and may sometimes do this for an audience larger than their colleagues. From the inflexible genealogy of France offered by Michelet and Lavisse, among others, to the fragmented version provided today by the *Lieux de mémoire*, they are responsible for the circulation of representations, arguments (whether explicit or not), and a repertoire of signs and forms which have been embodied in the shared culture since the nineteenth century. However, with two restrictions, there is nothing in this which constitutes a radically new departure in Western historiography.

The first important one is that the situations for which historical discourse must account have become complicated and diversified to an extraordinary degree since history began to be viewed as having intrinsic meaning (rather than being the purveyor of a collection of timeless moral, religious, and political cases), the national-identity claim became generalized, producing inseparable effects of affirmation and disintegration, decomposition and recomposition, and historians became aware that their instruments might prove unsuitable for accounting for these processes. How can one write the history of the former Yugoslavia? or that of the nations born out of its collapse at the beginning of the 1990s? And how, by the same token, can one retrospectively write the history of the Balkans (in which connection see Drago Roksandič's article)? What we have here is not just rival histories, each trying to gain acceptance for its primacy, its legitimacy, its values, but also argument-based narratives which often mobilize the same resources for conflicting ends, practising denial and revisionism on each other.[4] In terms of violence and instability, this is certainly an extreme situation? but who can fail to see that the erosion of grand narratives, national or more generally ideological, encourages the proliferation of individual histories which need no longer be compatible with each other?[5] Multiculturalism does not create these dramatic conditions by itself: at worst, it serves to express them. It is, however, quite obvious that it confronts historians with serious problems whose terms they are not prepared to accept. As for the identification of situations as extremes, it might perhaps be better to reserve this term for situations in which it has become difficult, if not impossible, to think satisfactorily in historical terms. If one follows Lucette Valensi, this applies to the Armenian question, about which she rightly points out that relativist precautions – everyone has his own truth – are no more acceptable, if only because of what is at stake in the debate, than the improbable solution of cobbling together a golden mean. But what is suggested by study of the conflicting historiography of the Armenian genocide is that it is a far more complex structure than the public recognizes and, moreover, that it is not always possible to separate the production of a body of knowledge about this past from the political appeals and implications which surround it and weigh it down. This may be seen as a way of pointing to the limits on what professional historians can think and write (a familiar tune), but it is also, more usefully, an invitation to reflect on the dynamic relationship between historical knowledge and the diverse forms of the public debate which must increasingly be negotiated.

For this is the second specificity of the contemporary debate: to a very great extent, it has become public, and professional historians are no longer in control of it. It is no coincidence that, since Jürgen Habermas put the term 'public use of history' into circulation during the *Historikerstreit*, the German historians' conflict about the significance of Nazism in their national experience, this expression has been constantly bandied about – first and foremost by specialists who have willingly made it their byword.[6] In using the phrase, it was the philosopher's intention, in a certain number of crucial cases which challenged values which are essential to the community, to break out of so-called specialist circles and submit the dispute to public debate. But what has happened in the last 25 years shows that the public use of history covers a far broader range of situations than this.[7] In forms which vary widely from one country to the next, there have been made attempts to reappropriate history 'from the bottom up', with proposals to groups at least – particularly those who have traditionally been deprived of the capacity to express themselves – to take part in mapping their own history. It is this which has given rise to the History Workshops movement in Great Britain, or the *Alltagsgeschichte* in Germany, as well as to the vast outpouring of eyewitness accounts, giving a voice to the anonymous, forgotten players, who have been silent or silenced: workers, women, immigrants, people on the margins of society, outlaws, exiles, and others. They have done this by inventing new forms and new places – workshops, magazines, publishing houses – off the beaten track of university institutions. And yet the initiative still came from professional historians. This is no more the case, however, and it is a well-known fact that often the subsequent impetus arose in an altogether different context. Is there any need to point out that the fact that if a start has finally been made on reconstructing the history of Vichy, it is due to the initial work of the American historian Robert Paxton and the Canadian historian Michael Marrus, but even more pertinently to the lengthy exercise of anamnesis performed by the film *Le Chagrin et la pitié* (1972)? If Touvier finally stood trial, if Bousquet could have been tried, if Papon was finally tried after so much reluctance, this was an outcome of the pressure of collective recollection far more than of the (necessary) work of the professional historians?[8] Writing in the context of the Italian example, Claudio Pavone draws attention to the development of the public use of history, or more specifically of the past, and invites historians to explore the history of this use too.

We have become almost familiar with such situations. They are not the only ones. At the same time we have seen historians bombarded with new requests: for expert opinions, to which we will return, which may come from the state, from major social institutions (such as the Catholic Church in the Touvier affair), but also by groups, or even individuals. At the same time in the United States there has come into being, more boldly than in France, a 'public history': an ambiguous definition, where perhaps the term of 'applied history' might be preferable. This involves professionals making their specialized knowledge and skills available to specific interests for what may be highly disparate ends: the history of a company commissioned by itself, or the search for a precedent, or the drawing up of an argument, the establishing of a case for the defence. It will be agreed it is not possible to claim that this type of request – sometimes a commission – does not, one way or the other, affect the historian's position and stance, even if the profession sometimes pretends that this is merely a normal extension of its recognized skills.

Not all these instances of interference in the public debate – or what is sometimes supposed to substitute for it – necessarily entail political uses of the past. It will, however, readily be agreed that neither do they exclude it, to say the least. And, in addition, the meaning of these uses must be agreed upon. Some are tantamount to straightforward manipulation. Revisionism and denial have for the last 25 years provided exacerbated and intolerable illustrations of this. Yet it should be remembered that history lends itself to forms of manipulation which are more discreet and hence more easily accepted. This can be attested to by the entire historiographic tradition, since it offers a unique possibility of mobilizing arguments of precedence and authority – even if it means actually going in search of them. These are not the most novel uses. In his contribution to this issue, Giovanni Levi draws attention to the extent to which historians are tempted to take for granted those interpretative outlines which are suggested to them by the too obvious achievements of the present, concluding, for example, that certain major phenomena are inescapable. Examples would include the advent of a single form for the modern state, the inevitability of a form of capitalism defined according to neo-liberal norms; descriptions intended to legitimate – or often to exalt – unity or, in contrast, separation within national entities, or alternatively to justify forms of power which often have very little to do with actual historical experiences. Levi rightly notes the extent to which professional historians sometimes seem to be lacking in critical perspectives and tools, and suggests that the epistemological turmoil affecting the social sciences on the one hand, and scholarly institutions on the other, has finished up by furthering, at both ends of the spectrum, a oversimplified confrontation between a historical shared meaning which is ill-founded and public opinion which is badly prepared. The current issue of *Enquête* seeks to contribute to a critical new start in this domain.

Lastly, among the political uses of the past we still have to classify those involving the historian's basic position in time – that is, his/her contemporaneousness and the historicity of his procedures. All of us keep repeating that history is a relationship between a present and a past, of which we are only familiar with the traces, but often (with a few notable exceptions, such as Marc Bloch's *L'Etrange défaite*) we fail to draw the consequences. This should be an opportunity to reflect on what it means, for a historian, to be the contemporary of the contemporary – a situation which, effectively, involves a political use of the past; to ask ourselves questions about the régime of historicity in which these questions arise.

A series of questions emerges from this exercise: some of them new, others very old, but today possessing a particular urgency and a redefined significance. Why today? It is worth dwelling briefly on this historiographic moment.

II

Let us here, in the shape of a few brief jottings, outline the present conjuncture, taking the French situation as our touchstone. We have no intention of overvaluing it, or of dealing with it as such, but rather intend simply to identify a number of concerns, themes, or keywords arising from it, as an aid to defining what is going on in the historical discipline or historians' workshops. The intention of this collection of essays is, by the same token, to help decipher the various cases which are presented and to pinpoint what is a translation or reformulation of the present circumstances, and what a deviation from them.

What new questions are facing the historian? What role is s/he requested to play, or asked not to play? Or would he not wish to play? Can he, albeit as yet tentatively, identify something new in his/her practice, epistemology, stance? These are, basically, those questions which count. If we were to use the analytical categories proposed by Reinhart Koselleck, we would focus on the meeting point between a change in experience (*Erfahrungswandel*) and changes in method (*Methodenwechsel*), as well as the inevitable gaps and discrepancies between the two.[9]

The rapid rise, followed by its primacy, of the 'contemporary' or the 'present' as a dominant category would be the first quality of these circumstances. Instead of the grand narratives, which have vanished, today there are 'key words', like the passwords of time. Taking one leads on to the others: if not a system, they constitute at the very least a network, or indeed even a dictionary of accepted ideas. One anticipates them, expects people to relate to them. The list can readily be produced: present, memory, identity, genocide, witness, responsibility will certainly be on it.

The contemporary is an imperative. Pressure, at least vague and sometimes very specific or emphatic, has been brought to bear in order for the social sciences to focus more on the contemporary and respond better, faster, to the 'social demand' – or even to anticipate it. In order to deal with this demand, experts are called upon: is the historian then perceived primarily as an *expert* in matters of memory?

In the historical discipline, this rise of the contemporary has been reflected in many forms: in course syllabuses, student numbers, and faculty positions; but also in the demand for and success of the expression 'the history of the present time'.[10] It is also noteworthy that the 'present' which is covered by 'the history of the present time' has been expanded. In 25 years, contemporary history has thus shifted from the discipline's margins to its centre. The 'other' histories – modern, medieval, ancient – which played a leading role and, during the 1970s and 1980s, constituted the face of history in the eyes of the public, enjoying a large audience, now appear to have retreated, to be less meaningful. As if what they must or can say found it difficult to permeate the increasingly thick layer of the *present*, as if the questions they were asking were by now unfamiliar to the public, which, caught up in the circle of the present, is obsessed with memory.

But the domain of the contemporary, where the historian is a mere latecomer, is largely occupied – by journalists, to start with. So who is to have what role, or what roles sharing is to occur, since the respective temporalities in which these people work and the resulting agenda are not the same? We are living in a time of high-speed – quasi-day-by-day – historicization of the present: can the historian also 'do live history', giving the posterity's point of view on the very day that events happen, and shooting faster than his shadow? Is this something he can do? – is this something he can refuse to do? In either case, what is the price which must be paid?

This rise has been accompanied by an intensification of the public use of the past, following the formula proposed by Jürgen Habermas at the time of the German historians' conflict, which was very specifically a public controversy played out on the pages of the Federal Republic's main newspapers. Use of the past? Actually, largely but not exclusively of this recent past, which does not 'pass', or alternatively of this 'present' (which also does not 'pass'). As we have found, this history is no more the exclusive of the professional historians. There are numerous players now. Among them, eyewitnesses are taking up more and more room, so much so that recently reference was made to the era of the eyewitness – *L'ère du témoin*.[11] Today, an eyewitness is first and foremost the voice and the face of a victim, of a survivor who is listened to, encouraged to speak, recorded, and filmed. The largest scale project underway is that of the Spielberg Foundation, which has the goal of collecting all the eyewitness testimony of all Nazi camp survivors. This gives rise to the question asked most frequently: Who is an historian, and who decides who reopens the file: the eyewitness or the historian? Is the eyewitness a 'source', or a 'voice' which is best heard 'online' without going through the mediation of the historian? The major 'waves' of French commemorative events, starting with the bicentennial of 1789, mark the cycle of public life, conjoining memories (forgotten, recalled, triggered, and so forth) and political agendas. Clearly, historians are not in control of the calendar, nor always of the questions or terms of the debates which are triggered by these celebrations, but it cannot be denied that they do have an impact on research directions and publishing programmes.

More recently, France's National Assembly adopted a legal motion on the Armenian genocide (28 May 1998), comprising a single article: 'France publicly acknowledges the Armenian genocide of 1915.' Having long been appealed to and entreated by Armenian activist associations, who finally managed to make themselves heard, do the legislators intend to fix history? The preamble begins as follows: 'Our country and the world's democracies have a pressing duty of memory. This memory cannot restrict itself to each nation's history. It must also expand to include the memory of humanity which has been tragically affected in the course of this century by several genocides.' The transition is made from the specific to the universal via the necessity of the duty of memory: from the memory of the Armenians to the memory of mankind, via the intermediary of the law. The legislators see themselves as not so much historians as teachers of memory.

This proposal (first proposed by members of parliament and not by the government), after being unanimously passed first by the National Assembly, then by the Senate and a second time by the Assembly, is now a law (18 January 2001). That means a tragic event (the genocide) which has no direct link with the country's own history, but which is acknowledged as underpinning not just an Armenian but a French-Armenian identity, is officially made part of French legislation. As if, in order to feel 'fully' French, the Armenian French also needed the solemn recognition of this right to memory (which would therefore become a duty of memory binding on everybody).

A final example of this political use of the past is to be found in yet another legal motion 'aiming at the recognition of the slave trade and slavery as crimes against humanity' (16 February 1999). The goal is for France to 'pay its respects to the memory of the victims of this crime of oppression'. Article 2 makes provision for textbooks to 'treat at length the longest and largest scale deportation in the history of mankind', while Article 5 stipulates that a committee will be empowered 'to examine the conditions for reparations due on account of this crime'. Whatever the final outcome of these texts, which at the time of writing have not been passed as bills and perhaps never will, they also have the merit of being symptomatic: showing how the legislators understand, adopt as their byword and, as it were, applies to themselves (in a spirit of secular repentance) 'the duty of memory'.[12]

This duty applies first and foremost precisely to crimes against humanity. Defined by the legislator, crimes against humanity were submitted to judges before the historians of the present time were confronted by their original temporality: there is no passing of time, since the criminal remains ever contemporary of his crime. 'Inherently' falling outside the purview of the statute of limitations, crimes against humanity embody 'a legal atemporality which is alien to the time dealt with by history'.[13]

On this ground of the contemporary, historians often encounter journalists, sometimes legislators, and in addition have dealings with judges: directly or indirectly, actually or metaphorically speaking. This last encounter is not their own doing, but it does of course tie in with the conspicuous and striking judicialization of the public sphere: judges now decide on everything, 'curing' public and private ills, past and present, if not future. People talk about judicial 'therapy'. Which means, in history, reopening another issue, that of 'the judge and the historian', and striking interferences between history and the judiciary.[14] People may no longer refer to or speak in the name of the judgement of history, but on the other hand there is a proliferation of questions about judges and historians: whether a judge passing sentence, or, more frequently, an examining magistrate in the inquisitorial French system. With a reappraisal, in this light, of the thoughts about proof and the concept of context. On the other hand, the question of a historical judgement has remained in the background.

There has been a flourishing of more or less formal or official commissions of historians (the least formal, but far from the least in terms of attracting media coverage, or the least problematic, being the 'Aubrac round table' in the spring of 1997[15]), as well as commissions made up of historians and jurists (such as the Matteoli mission on the looting of French Jewry). And, lastly, a number of trials – on charges of crimes against humanity – were designed as moments of memory (it should be possible for the victims' complaints to be spoken, heard, and receive a form of reparation), but they were also to function and above all to remain as 'instruments of history' (which is why the proceedings were recorded[16]). Moreover, they posed the specific question about the historian's presence as a witness, a witness by virtue of his expertise, certainly, but nevertheless a 'witness' (as defined in the French Code of Criminal Procedure) all the same.

Caught up in the circumstances outlined here, what has been the response of historians, and first of all of those in the front line, the historians of the present time? They have agreed to take part, here and there, in commissions of historians; they have issued reminders of the rules of the profession, as well as calls to act responsibly.[17] This was to be one of the major themes of the 19th International Congress of the Historical Sciences held in Oslo in August 2000, 'Uses and Abuses of History and the Historian's Responsibility, Present and Past'. Are such reminders, indicating uneasiness but also perhaps withdrawal, sufficient, and what should be the 'social role' of the 'responsible' historian?

Translated by Ruth Morris

NOTES

1. P. Novick, *That Noble Dream. The 'Objectivity Question' and the American Historical Profession* (Cambridge, 1988). For France, see W.R. Keylor, *Academy and Community. The Foundation of the French Historical Profession* (Cambridge, MA, 1975).
2. J. Revel, 'Le fardeau de la mémoire', *Correspondances*, 55 (1999), pp.3–9.
3. This is also, of course, the problem facing those historians who had to provide a link between the Israeli present and the biblical past. On the role of Hebrew in this process, see, for example, B. Harshav, *Language in Time of Revolution* (Berkeley, 1993).
4. On the possibilities which the decomposition/recomposition of historiographic reference narratives offers revisionism (in the meaning normally associated with this term), see the recent special report which *Les Temps modernes* (606, Nov.–Dec. 1999) published on the new 'readings' of the genocide of the Jews in Hungary and Romania.
5. On a specific instance, see M. Kriegel, 'Un programme multiculturel pour Israël? Les "nouveaux historiens"', *Le Débat*, 104 (1999), pp.149–61. See also I. Greilsammer, *La nouvelle histoire d'Israël. Essai sur une identité nationale* (Paris, 1998).
6. *Devant l'histoire* (Paris, 1987).
7. Cf. N. Gallerano (ed.), *L'uso publico della storia* (Milan, 1995); idem, *La verità della storia. Sull' uso publico del passato* (Rome, 1999); idem, 'Histoire et usage public de l'histoire', *Diogène*, 168 (1994), pp.87–106. In Italy, it was the questions raised by R. de Felice's bibliography of Mussolini and those who commented on it which sparked off this discussion.
8. Nevertheless, it may happen that it is a historian who, by applying his skills, alerts public opinion to the state of a case file. One such example is Pierre Vidal-Naquet over the revisionist theses on the genocide of the Jews during World War II ('Un Eichmann de papier', *Esprit* (Sept. 1980)); another is Carlo Ginzburg, who took the documents from the case papers and redid the pretrial investigation of the Soffri case in order to show the contradictions in the charges (*Il Giudice e lo storico* (Turin, 1991)).
9. R. Koselleck, *L'expérience de l'histoire* (Paris, 1997).
10. The Institut d'histoire du temps présent was set up by the CNRS in 1978.
11. A. Wiewiorka, *L'ère du témoin* (Paris, 1998); F. Hartog, 'Le témoin de l'historien', *Gradhiva*, 27 (2000), pp.1–4.
12. In a last example, the National Assembly unanimously approved (28 Feb. 2000) a legal motion to establish a 'title of Righteous of France' and to introduce 'a national day to commemorate the victims of the racist and antisemitic crimes of the French State and to pay tribute to the Righteous of France'.
13. Y. Thomas, 'La vérité, le temps, le juge, l'historien', *Le Débat*, 102 (Nov.–Dec. 1998), p.29.
14. See the entire special report entitled 'Vérité judiciaire, vérité historique', ibid., pp.4–51.
15. This 'round table' brought together on the premises of the *Libération* newspaper Mr and Mrs Aubrac and a number of historians (see *Libération*, 9 July 1997). Raymond and Lucie Aubrac wanted to have this meeting with the professional historians of the period in order to put an end, once and for all, to the accusations of treason disseminated about Raymond Aubrac and relating to the arrests carried out in Caluire on 21 June 1943 (arrest of Jean Moulin, but also of Raymond Aubrac). The historians present unanimously acknowledged this formally to them. Things could have been left there. But this strange round table continued and then shifted into trial mode. What was actually introduced was a logic of

crossexamination and admissions: the foolhardiness demonstrated by Lucie Aubrac in trying to get her husband released was construed as misdeeds; Raymond Aubrac was asked to explain why the Germans did not transfer him to Paris, and to justify the variations (which had become 'contradictions') in his successive statements about these few months.

16. At the time of writing, in the autumn of 2000 the History Channel on cable TV has broadcast some of the recordings of the trial of Klaus Barbie.
17. See the special report published by the *Diogène* journal, 168 (1994), entitled 'La responsabilité sociale de l'historien'. In his article, F. Bédarida refers to an combination of three functions: critical, civic, ethical.

Towards an Ethnographic Phenomenology of the Greek Spirit

MICHAEL HERZFELD

Greece is a country about which many have waxed eloquent and about which many of the most eloquent have displayed appalling ignorance. Everyone, it seems, knows 'what Greece is', but few have cared to ask the Greeks in a way that would encourage intimate reflection rather than eliciting the views promoted by the self-appointed guardians of the classical mantle. The latter are anxious to safeguard their privileged status as the representatives of a foreign cultural and political hegemony, and, through the educational system, they have ensured at least a veneer of harmonious compliance. Here lies the main contribution that a specifically anthropological perspective may be able to offer: the *ethnography* of daily responses to official discourse about the past may differ radically from what we have been taught to believe by those with real power. Such an ethnography will show that the stereotypes of Hellene and *Romios* (the Greek as descendant of glorious ancient forebears and the Greek as the rather compromised heir to Byzantine, Turkish, Arabic, and Slavic cultural traits, all of them essentialized in an equally uncompromising fashion) are not mutually exclusive alternatives one of which must be the true account of what it means to be Greek but strategic devices through which ordinary people deploy and yet also are consumed by official ideologies – a complex dialectic to which there is no obvious resolution.[1]

Because Greece occupied a position in the European colonial imagination out of all proportion to its size or political influence, its ancient heritage was a matter of deep concern to the Great Powers. The 'liberation' of Greece from the Turkish 'yoke' was effected in such a way as to leave the newly constituted country heavily dependent on its ability to present as indigenous an ancient culture that most of its inhabitants experienced as foreign and preternaturally strange, while an entrenched and Western-oriented elite continued the work of cultural refashioning from within as the best means of maintaining its own, foreign-supported authority. The long stream of post-World War II military governments and the colonels' dictatorship of 1967–74 were but the most obvious signs of this internalization of hegemony.

The negotiation of the Greek past is both a reflection and a distortion of larger projects still occurring in the encompassing space of post-Enlightenment Europe. Greece, the supposed ancestor of the European spirit, was also reconstituted out of an allegedly corrupt, barbaric, and profoundly Oriental morass in which the very rudiments of culture were lacking. The Greeks found themselves cast as citizens of a nation-state that was supposed to represent the 'regeneration' of a Hellas invented to a significant degree by German classical philologists in the late eighteenth and early nineteenth centuries. The Greek political leadership, which owed its domestic prestige and power to its subservience abroad, energetically promoted a programme of cultural refashioning that has continued, with some reversals and modifications, until very recently – indeed, continues to echo, albeit with increasing hollowness, in the pronouncements of politically and culturally conservative segments of the elite.

This was the public face presented by Greek officialdom at least until the collapse of Greek ambitions in Asia Minor in 1922 and again with the fitful but often brutal reassertion of right-wing power for over half a century more, up to the ignominious collapse of the colonels' dictatorship in 1974. The logic of the association between right-wing politics and this emphasis on the classical heritage is not hard to find: Hellas was the cultural touchstone of European inclusion, its academic and intellectual guardianship was in the hands of countries far more powerful than those of the Greek state, and the apparent alternatives – first, reversion to Ottoman control; later, surrender to the 'Slavic dogma' of communism – would have spelled disaster for a bourgeois state the authority of which was grounded in the mutual equivalence of law and order, civilization, and Hellenism. Those who argue that outbreaks of ethnic strife in the Balkans are the product of some inherited predisposition to chaotic violence would do well to reflect on the fact that the first Balkan nation state and the site of one of its bloodiest civil wars was conceived as a product of Enlightenment rationalism and Romantic essentialism – the latter in effect creating a template for the self-reproducing pattern of 'ethnonationalism' that Stanley Tambiah and Robert Hayden have probed with particular acuity.[2] In the escalating chain reaction of ethnogenesis, Hellas – with Western endorsement – has represented itself as a pool of calm, European culture with internal resources of venerable age and impeccable lineage. The price for this has, of course, been its continuing subjection to the silent colonialism of the Western powers in their confrontation with Soviet power in the rest of the Balkans. Only with the collapse of the communist regimes of eastern Europe and the sudden rise (much favoured by powerful elements in Russia and Serbia) of Greek neo-Orthodox fundamentalism has this dualistic structure begun to unravel; but then that is the continuing story of much of the world.

The Greeks' misfortune was to internalize this dualism – first as the civilized West versus the barbaric East, then as the free West versus the repressive East – so that, official statements to the contrary, its two elements have coexisted in uneasy tension for virtually all of modern Greek history. The official state may have tried to do away with much that was familiar in everyday life, and to a remarkable degree it succeeded. But it also forced educated proponents of a more nativistic, 'realist' culture into a comparable form of essentialism, reproducing as a debate between opposed ideological camps a phenomenon that Jean Jackson has recently noted for minority ethnicities struggling against authoritarian forms of state nationalism.[3]

This was a reaction against a vision that treated virtually the entire gamut of everyday culture as potentially foreign and therefore subversive. It came fitfully and in forms that were not always recognizable as such: the dominant political culture was extraordinarily literal-minded, as perhaps befitted a system dedicated to the stabilization of a single cultural vision, and could not cope with allusion, allegory, or ambiguity. One sees a process developing in which this intolerance of uncertain meanings gradually crept into the rhetoric and ideology of the opposition as it became more vocal, a process that was doubtless also hastened by its association with left-wing political movements sympathetic to the equally humourless Soviet Union.[4] Again, the Greeks in this regard were internalizing processes taking place on a world stage, but their peculiar entailment in the ideological history of 'the West' as an idea and a political force made them do so in ways that make the Greek case an exemplary site for research on the politics of the past.

The opposed strains of Enlightenment Eurocentrism and reactive ethnocentrism have actually coalesced, but only when the political left wing attained power. Then, in a move that parallels similar phenomena in language, the left may have felt constrained to demonstrate its allegiance to the Hellenic ideals that it had hitherto derided in its nationalistic foes on the right: it is surely no coincidence that it was Melina Mercouri, Minister of Culture in the first post-1974 socialist government of Andreas Papandreou, who both led the campaign to demand the return of the Elgin Marbles to Greece and introduced a measure whereby Greeks (including foreigners able to demonstrate Greek descent) would be exempt from museum and archaeological site charges to be levied on all non-Greek travellers. The argument was that Greeks themselves were not visiting these repositories of 'their' heritage – an argument in which biogenetic racism and embarrassment at what was seen as a national 'failure' were mixed in roughly equal parts. This was also the period in which even the relatively leftist government of Papandreou – which did, after all, govern a European Union country – came to see that it could not wield power for long without experiencing the imperatives of the classical heritage. These compromises reproduce earlier attempts to reconcile the pagan Hellenism of the state with the orthodox Christianity of its associated church – an example of syncretism that, as Charles Stewart sagely notes, carries over into political life.[5]

This, in broad outline, is the political context in which the vagaries of historicism in Greece will now be examined. An account of this sort is necessarily crude, and it ignores some reversals of the pattern described here that occurred in various localities and at various times. Nevertheless, it is striking that the pattern throughout Greek history is consistent, in sharp contrast – as indicated below – with the situation in Italy. It is therefore appropriate to turn now to some of the details of the representation of the past that are especially indicative of the processes involved.

SIGNS OF A DIFFERENT PAST

As I have already indicated, the Greeks' experience of battles over the past represents one of the less well known consequences of colonialism. Very few parts of Greece were actually occupied militarily by the West for any length of time; Western leaders diverted attention from the colonial character of their role in Greece by emphasizing the antecedent 'occupation' of 'Greece' by the Turks – a construction that retrospectively casts the present-day map of the Greek nation-state back in time, ignoring the multiethnic character of the *entire* Ottoman Empire including the segment today known as Greece and suppressing the equally inconvenient fact that there had hitherto never existed a Greek national entity as such – unless we accept the modern Greek claim that the Macedonians Philip and Alexander, heartily disliked by the Athenians of their time for their imperialistic successes, should now be unequivocally recanonized as true Greeks and recast as the saviours of the transcendent Greek spirit of democracy.

It is well known that the European imperialists studied the classics as a source of models and insight.[6] What is less well known is that they reimported their vision of Greece back into that land itself in ways that conflated local specificities of the past to serve the homogenizing logic of the present: Lord Guilford, presiding over the Ionian Academy on Corfu – one of the few places actually occupied by another European nation in the modern era – and clad in his reconstructed ancient dress supposedly in the manner of Socrates, is the sartorial equivalent of the Bavarian architects' reclassicization of Athens, hitherto a partly Albanian-speaking backwater, through the erection of such buildings as the Old Parliament and Palace and the Zappeion.[7] (More unkindly, perhaps, we might recall that Corfu is, along with the Trobriand Islands in New Guinea, one of the few places to have retained a version of cricket from the days of the British *imperium*.) Clothing, architecture, and a visibly rationalistic discipline of the body were the physical loci, from the body personal to the body politic, of a new cultural idiom that was both liberating and enslaving – a revival of 'tradition' as an effective tool of both internal and external domination in the name of 'civilization'. It is not that there were no continuities with antiquity; the language alone is powerful testimony to the perseverance of local cultural forms, while the Orthodox Church often recast ancient deities in the guise of Christian saints, permitting a certain continuity in the forms of worship while denying the persistence of 'paganism'. But the specific choices that the foreign philhellenes made focused on those aspects of the classical past that reproduced their own vision of a great civilization, and these were not always the elements that had persisted in the most recognizable way at the local level or in everyday life. Moreover, the assumption that cultural continuities indicated the persistence of some kind of collective memory seems to have resulted in a peculiarly neoclassical rendition of the idea of 'national consciousness' that is still very much a part of, especially, the more conservative forms of Greek nationalist rhetoric.

Much has been made in the literature of the conflicting images of Greek culture: the 'Hellenes' as quintessential Europeans, the Romii as the inheritors of Turkish and Byzantine influences. In the emergent confrontation between Eurocentrists and nativists, these models of Greekness acquired growing significance and progressively became more sharply – and, from an ethnographic point of view, more selectively – defined.

Yet the syncretistic arrangements that have emerged in our own times – first, the colonels' adoption of the idea that pagan religion in Greece anticipated the philosophical tenets of Christianity, then the socialists' nationalistic Hellenism – exhibited a degree of internal strain because they were always attempts to iron out plural origins for a unitary present (the perennial problem of virtually all nationalisms). Nineteenth century historians such as Paparrhegopoulos and Zambelios lauded the 'Hellenic Christian civilization' of the Greeks, seeking thereby to obscure the inconvenient circumstance that, to the Byzantine (and Christian) world that immediately preceded the period of Turkish domination, for most Greek speakers 'Hellenes' were pagans, while to the people of the countryside they were a race of giants – in either case, in other words, alien to the Christian and Greek speaking world of more recent times.[8] The attempt to yoke these mutually hostile strands of the national heritage together – which was aggressively pursued by the dictator George Papadopoulos in his slogan

'Greece of the Hellenic Christians' – belongs, as I have noted elsewhere,[9] to a classic strain in both the authoritarian discourse of nationalism and, more generally, the mythopoetic toolbox of modern nationalisms.

Papadopoulos himself embodied many of the contradictions that this device was intended to scramble into invisibility. First, while he mandated the use of the neoclassical purist language (*katharevousa*) in education, government, and the (state-censored) media, he himself spoke it with impressive incompetence. Moreover, the extremist and religious society to which he and others of the regime belonged, Zoï ('Life'), was, as the philosopher-theologian Christos Yannaras (Giannaras) has wryly observed, a fundamentally *Protestant* organization at base, inimical to the antirationalist and non-Cartesian worldview espoused by adherents of older forms of Byzantine doctrinal orthodoxy.[10] (It may be significant that, to this day, successive Greek governments have found themselves embarrassed by the radical religiosity of the Old Calendrists; although the latter are often popularly regarded as 'more religious' than the established, official Orthodox Church, their insistence on retaining the old calendar conflicts with the modernizing rhetoric and practices of the latter and appears to challenge the purity of its teachings.)

The colonels were heirs to the same impetus towards bureaucratization and the reduction of ambiguity as the proponents of an equally tendentious reading of the classical past – the neoclassicists originally imported by the Bavarian court of the first king, Otho. Thus, attempts to resolve these paradoxes of the past through the formulation, originally proposed by Claude Fauriel in 1824,[11] of syncretistic paradoxes must always struggle with a logic of state that is fundamentally inimical to anything that smacks of compromise, miscegenation (whether genetic or cultural), or ambiguity. The Greek bourgeoisie must collude in the invention of a European past for itself, yet that collusion shackles it to the very qualities that have at times invited Western sneers about medieval values and cultural fakery.

Such contortions in the management of the past are closely related – although not in a simple way – to the Greeks' often tense engagements with their country's immediate neighbours. The denial of the existence of a Macedonian minority, for example, is commonly assumed to be a reflection of fears about Turkish manipulation of Macedonian sentiment, and this is certainly an important part of the picture. But it is equally significant that Greek politicians have long felt the need to claim Macedonia as an integral part of what we might call the 'prehistory' of the Greek state. It is important to keep these details in mind when contemplating present day struggles over the definition of the past in Greece.

Such are the considerations of *Realpolitik* – the aspect most usually acknowledged by political scientists. But there is also the dangerous fit between popular categories and the hard language of strident ethnonationalism – in Greece as much as in neighbouring countries. While there are many intellectuals in Greece today who have spoken against such essentializing of difference in terms of ancestry and imported models of Europeanness and have criticized the official refusal to recognize ethnic variation where it so clearly exists, theirs are only a few voices, however significant, and they are often accused in the popular press of treachery and dishonesty, so successful has been the permeation of the popular imagination by the logic of the state.[12]

One consequence of this has been the continuing drumbeat of praise to 'our ancient past'. Speak of Macedonia – an especially contentious issue – and you raise the spectres of Philip and Alexander. And, as has recently been observed, the current intense political unease over the national birth rate (which is in sharp decline) reflects ongoing conflict with Turkey, a conflict that is again frequently invested with moral validity by its overtones of 'defending civilization'. Those few souls – human rights activists, feminists, and some hardy academics – who have dared to oppose this predominant logic are brave indeed, and their voices may be exerting some long-term influence, but for the moment they are not the voices that speak for Greece in the international media and they are still hesitant in the arenas of diplomacy and cultural exchange.

Yet here a word about numbers is in order – especially because one of the commonest defences of the official position is that the minority populations are too small to warrant the risk of territorial claims by other countries that recognizing them might provoke. Other voices, too, are few but surely significant – no less 'Greek' than the majority view in each case.

Let us turn for illustration to an example drawn directly from the contestation of local history that occurs in the context of resistance to official forms of historic conservation. In Rethemnos, Crete, women who contest their husbands' claims to their shared homes as 'patropaternal' are not only dismissing both these patriarchal claims of authority over what from the wives' perspective is dower property inherited from their mothers rather than transmitted from their fathers to their husbands. They are also joining their husbands in rejecting an official view of these houses as monuments of national identity and thus as in some sense the common heritage of an entire nation allegedly represented by the bureaucratic state. And they are prefiguring feminist objections to the race-based, classicizing view of Hellenic identity by suggesting that the bloodline does not necessarily define what is 'ours'. It is not even clear that such views are numerically rare; but in any case they clearly do articulate sentiments that connect them with present day social currents in Greece, and the argument that they are marginal or unrepresentative will not wash.[13]

The argument in Rethemnos concerns, at base, the question of whether a domestic quarter, however beautiful, should be treated as a 'national monument' rather than as a human dwelling. In extreme cases, notably in Japan and Korea, even individual human beings – artists and craftspeople of rare distinction – may be treated as national treasures. But in a culture such as that of Greece, in which monumentality appears to be *opposed* in the popular imagination to the social life of ordinary people, in which the 'studied performance of spontaneity' holds centre stage, and in which there is a powerful popular tendency to oppose the state (*kratos*) to the nation (*ethnos*), the temporal, symbolic, and ideological fixity implied by the very idea of the monument appears as an outrage to many.

The conceptual centrality of the monument in the Greek nationalist imagination goes back to the foundation of the state and is clearly connected to the Bavarian monarchy's early promotion of neoclassicism. The national Archaeological Service emerged in the first years of the young state's existence and has been a formidable political force ever since. Like Israel, which similarly grounds claims to territory on the concrete remnants of a past reclaimed for the new nation as its own, Greece has had every interest in pursuing the logic of a materiality that at one stroke gives it physical presence, temporal depth, and a claim to have achieved the most durable civilizational forms of all – a deliberate and successful promotion, as it were, of the fallacy of misplaced concreteness. Moreover, the important role of folklore in the creation of Greek national identity was explicitly and magisterially brought by Nikolaos Politis into the embrace of the same logic through his articulation of the view of folklore as 'monuments of the word' – a formulation that permitted the supposed reconstruction of 'original' and therefore authoritative texts through an application of stemmatics, the technique whereby philologists established chronological genealogies of interrelated manuscripts.[14] Not only was this strategy consistent with the bureaucratic literalism of the state but it also appeared to bring the vagrant orality of village lore under the control of a literary aesthetic. Ultimately, moreover, it enabled Politis and others to subsume folk memories of the Byzantine past, with its rich mixtures of cultural traditions, under the unyieldingly Hellenic image of a 'national epic' – a master stroke of hegemonic syncretism in the sense outlined here.

This had important consequences for the representation of the relationship between the Greek state and its neighbours. Politis' successor in the Chair of Hellenic Folklore at the University of Athens saw ethnology thus conceived as a valuable weapon with which to defend Greek cultural primacy in the region. Thus, George Megas explicitly denied the Bulgarians their own claims to a national epic by claiming all the available candidates to be poor imitations of 'the' Byzantine epic. At the same time, he derived all Balkan architecture from a rather hypothetical ancient Greek model, the *megaron*; his findings were published by the Ministry of Reconstruction, an important government agency charged with eliminating the enormous physical damage wrought by the Civil War and attributed by it exclusively to the 'anti-Hellenic' and 'pro-Slav' communists.[15] Reconstruction is as much a conceptual as it is a material, architectural issue under such conditions, and its engagement with the researches of one of Greece's premier nationalist folklorists indicates the depth of the commitment the state made to the restoration of a Hellenocentric European past. That reconstruction was already actively pursued in the architectural traditions brought by the early advisers to the Bavarian monarchy with which Greece was saddled at independence: *megaron* was also the title of virtually every imposing public building in the neoclassical style erected in Athens during those years and later. To borrow briefly from the Byzantinist neo-Orthodox perspective of writers such as Yannaras: a truly 'Protestant' architectural discipline ushered in the bureaucratization of identity that was also to lead to a complex and rigid classification of all cultural idioms, repressing as it did so the creative performativity of those forms in the name, ironically, of a proud and independent Greek 'spirit' (*pnevma*; cf. German *Geist*).

SOME THOUGHTS ABOUT HISTORIC CONSERVATION IN GREECE TODAY

This classificatory grid was soon extended over the inhabited spaces of modern Greece. In the first phase, all traces of the Turkish presence were either demolished or allowed to fall into disrepair. While a few mosques remained intact even after the departure of most Muslims in 1924, and while some individuals retained the characteristic *kafasia* or lattice work that functioned architecturally on the characteristically Turkish window-boxes (*kioskia*) for sentimental reasons or because they lacked the funds to carry out major remodelling, a significant part of the Ottoman experience was literally demolished. With the advent of prosperity under the colonels, domestic architecture in the neoclassical style – originally a bourgeois adaptation to and celebration of the values of imported Hellenism – was the next to go: because they were old they were also 'backward', and therefore – for such are the ironies of heritage politics – implicitly Turkish, even though their stylistic inspiration had originally been intended to *conceal* supposedly 'Turkish' interiors. (Here the popular disdain for anything old actually served the project of constantly updating the ancient: European modernity was held to be the ultimate achievement of classical civilization!) It took a further massive increase in the degree of leisure enjoyed by the bourgeoisie before its members could go beyond advertising its freedom from manual labour through the bodily device of the long fingernail to collecting ostentatiously useless memorabilia of that hitherto despised past – the remnants of which would have had little chance of such prestige, according to Michael Thompson's 'rubbish theory',[16] had they not first been dismissed as signs of a backwardness that had, indeed, rendered them sufficiently useless to provide the distinctive marks of a leisured identity. In this phase, too, even the Archaeological Service, sometimes quite grudgingly, finds itself constrained to preserve some of the remnants of the Turkish past. And besides, there is also the economic incentive of tourism, with its inbuilt exoticism – a further challenge to the state's capacity for syncretism, given the Western equation of the exotic with the oriental. (It is surely significant in this regard that the appearance of Middle Eastern belly dancers in Greek restaurants and nightclubs appears to have emanated from Chicago.) The problem for modernity is that it must always find a way of accommodating the past, if only in order to legitimize the present, and this, over the years, has given the nativists an ever-increasing purchase on the politics of identity.

Partly as a result of this progression, the Archaeological Service became increasingly involved in the preservation of the entire heritage rather than monuments of classical or older date alone. But this has brought it only heightened problems. Because of the way in which its mission was originally conceived, it seems systemically resistant to any serious engagement with the social problems caused by its intervention. Expanding the kinds of 'monument' that must be incorporated into its celebration of the national heritage has simply made the Service all the more visibly just another arm of the interfering, alien institution that so many Greeks find the state bureaucracy to be.

At best this expansion seems to have entailed a vague notion that certain rustic architectural styles that were neither neoclassical nor obviously Islamic in orientation constituted an indeterminate but valuable zone of tradition. Yet even the creation of new categories such as 'traditional neighbourhood' (*paradhosiaki sinikia*) has not really helped very much. The impetus behind this designation appears to have involved some recognition that monumentality was not a feature of domestic architecture – but the concept of 'tradition' employed here is as static, as disconnected from human experience, as that of 'monument'. It still leaves decisions about the physical appearance of a communal space in the hands of external bureaucrats rather than in those of residents. This is the other face of syncretism: its routinization as a means of achieving societal discipline through the control of domestic space. And here the long-vaunted 'free spirit' of the Greeks undercuts the rationalistic models invented by the bureaucratic state. While Greeks may indeed perform spontaneity, as indicated, they may often do so against the state itself, utilizing its own terms and concepts to reject the very possibility of state intervention in the lived environment – much, in fact, as Greeks will utilize the teachings of the church in order to attack the venality of its representatives, the priests. One aspect of spontaneity as locally conceived is the art of using officialdom's tools against itself – an example of this is the sheep-thief who invites the police to dinner, only to inform them at the end that alas! they have now eaten the evidence of the crime – and the ability to do so in the context of historic conservation pits processes of social action against categories of official culture.

COMPARATIVE OBSERVATIONS

The contrast between Greece and Italy, twin pillars of the classical tradition in the modern European topographical imagination, in terms of their present day constructions of identity could hardly be sharper. Indeed, that contrast, associated as it is with vast differences of wealth and power, tells its own story of the dangers that await any country forced to play the role of living ancestor to others more powerful on the global stage.

Although both Greece and Italy have been marginalized by more powerful European countries seeking to subjugate their interests to the vision of an easily controllable ancestral land, they differ strikingly in their political evolution. Greece to this day remains very much a client state, beholden to the West, whether in the form of the North Atlantic Treaty Organization and the United States during earlier times or as a second-tier member of the European Union today, whereas Italy is a member of the G-8 group of economic powers and exercises a strong political presence in several arenas of world affairs and international cultural politics. Greece exhibits a strongly centripetal sense of culture flow and its historiography recognizes but a single point of departure, that of Athens in the fifth century BC; in Italy every small *paese* is its own Athens. In Greece, minoritarian and dialectal identity interests are either ignored or suppressed; in Italy they receive strong support even from official sources. And in Greece the responsiveness to social context that marks at least the theory of historic conservation in Italy is largely absent; in its place there reigns a literalistic regime of reconstructing the world of antiquity 'as it was'.

Yet how do we know 'how it was'? When the local authorities in Rethemnos demanded that all houses in a given street should be painted the same colour, not only were they riding roughshod over present day values of individualistic self-expression but they were presuming a homogeneity that probably did not exist in Venetian times (even assuming that we can speak of that period as possessing the degree of aesthetic stability that such an attribution would require). House decoration expresses divisions and alliances internal to a living community; no wonder the good citizens of Rethemnos were so outraged by the presumption that they were living in a 'monument'.[17]

But we should not suppose that their opposition to state intervention made them particularly hostile to the national interest. Quite to the contrary, their capacity to oppose the state bureaucracy was couched in terms of the ideal-typical vision of the independently minded Greek hero, an indomitable opponent of authority for whom the national government itself was an imposition of foreign origin (as, of course, historically it was). Because Greeks can beat the state at its own game in their evocation of such national self-stereotypes, they do not – and in this they are quite unlike Italians – find it necessary to doubt the fundamental unity of their nation. They are simply, in the segmentary logic they employ, the *best* of Greeks. But by the same token they are not only heroic individualists but also Orientalized atomists, allegedly incapable of economic progress without the tutelage of those who have written them into this fatalistic assessment of their national character.

For that very reason, it becomes clear, they do not consider their own historical experience to be that of the state. As do Italians, they see tax evasion and opposition to the conservation authorities as two laudable pursuits; but whereas in Italy this is seen as resistance to Rome, in Greece it is seen as the result of the corruption of Athens by outside forces; even the government is 'foreign'. For Greeks, Athens remains the centre, and their arguments against the particular idiom of bureaucratic intervention in their dwelling places adopts the rhetoric of the centre. Mischievously and effectively, they refute the demands of the centre with its own rhetoric (much as they attack the church in the language of its own doctrinal attitude to venality). But as a result they remain trapped in the logic of that rhetoric, which is why, when national crisis looms, and despite (for example) the Cretans' contempt for Greek Macedonians as Slavicized and in every way impure fellow-citizens, they will take to the streets and the battlefield in unequivocal, unanimous displays of solidarity. Segmentation allows them to have their localist cake and consume it as a national diet as well. But this saps their ability to play a leading role on the international stage, as their frequent humiliation in the European Union attests (although to a decreasing degree at the time of writing).

We are gradually beginning to see how the local-level discourse of identity, so often in overt conflict with the discourse of nationalist historiography, actually supports it in Greece. The lived experience – the *vioma* – of Greeks facing the potential conflict of interest between local place and nation is actually a space for the negotiation of relative identities.

Here, all identities are expressed in absolute terms. But just as the apparently strict sexual and social morality of traditional Greek society turns out to have provided the rhetorical cover for a wide range of possible ways of acting, so too the confluence of two seemingly rigid systems – state bureaucracy and the popular ethnosemantics of race and blood – actually permits the negotiability that mandates hospitality to the worst of enemies and distrust of the best of friends. In such a social setting, the very language of a literalistic, neoclassicist historiography grounded in the philology of eighteenth century Germany and undergirded by a century and a half of authoritarian pedagogy actually provides the tool-kit whereby ordinary people, unschooled though they may be, find themselves possessing both the means of their temporary emancipation from such an all-enveloping past and the shackles that, in the long term and on the larger stage, bind them to it.

NOTES

1. For a fuller account of these stereotypes, see my discussions in *Ours Once More: Folklore, Ideology, and the Making of Modern Greece* (Austin, 1982); *Anthropology through the Looking-Glass: Critical Ethnography in the Margins of Europe* (Cambridge, 1987); and *Cultural Intimacy: Social Poetics in the Nation-State* (New York, 1997).
2. Robert Hayden, 'Imagined Communities and Real Victims: Self-Determination and Ethnic Cleansing in Yugoslavia', *American Ethnologist*, 23 (1996), pp.73–801; Stanley J. Tambiah, 'Ethnic Conflict in the World Today', *American Ethnologist*, 16 (1989), pp.335–49.
3. Jean E. Jackson, 'Culture, Genuine and Spurious: The Politics of Indianness in the Vaupés, Colombia', *American Ethnologist*, 22 (1995), pp.3–27.
4. Although this is not the appropriate place for such a discussion, the role of the geopolitical division of the world between Marxist and capitalist juggernauts in overdetermining ethnicities in the Balkan region is a fascinating topic. To take just one example, it is clear that both the emergence of a distinctive Macedonian identity and the Greek reactions to it were intensified by an assumed equation of communism with 'Slavic dogma'. See Anastasia Karakasidou, *Fields of Wheat, Hills of Blood: Passages to Nationhood in Greek Macedonia, 1870–1990* (Chicago, 1997); Loring M. Danforth, *The Macedonian Conflict: Ethnic Nationalism in a Transnational World* (Princeton, 1995); and, for an earlier phase in the emergence of this ideological taxonomy, Herzfeld, *Ours Once More*, p.57.
5. Charles Stewart, 'Syncretism and a Dimension of Nationalist Discourse in Modern Greece', in Charles Stewart and Rosalind Shaw (eds.), *Syncretism/Anti-Syncretism: The Politics of Religious Synthesis* (London, 1994), pp.127–44.
6. See, notably, Christopher Stray, *Classics Transformed: Schools, Universities, and Society in England, 1830–1960* (Oxford, 1998); Richard Symonds, *Oxford and Empire: The Last Lost Cause?* (Houndsmills, 1986).
7. *Ours Once More,* p.35; William St. Clair, *That Greece Might Still Be Free: The Philhellenes in the War of Independence* (London, 1972), p.21; and, in more detail, G.P. Henderson, *The Ionian Academy* (Edinburgh, 1988), pp.21–2.
8. *Ours Once More*, pp.125–8.
9. See *Anthropology through the Looking-Glass*, p.181.
10. See Christos Yannaras, *Orthodhoksia ke dhisi: I theoloyia stin Elladha simera* (Athens, 1972) and *Orthodhoksia ke dhisi sti neoteri Elladha* (Athens, 1992).

11. Claude Fauriel, *Chansons populaires de la Grèce moderne*, Vol. 1 (Paris, 1824). See also Herzfeld, *Ours Once More*, pp.97–122; Alki Kyriakidou-Nestoros, *I theoria tis ellinikis laoghrafias: Kritiki analisi* (Athens, 1978), pp.91–7.
12. See, notably, Andonis Liakos (ed.), *O Ianos tou ethnikismou ke i elliniki valkaniki politiki* (Athens, 1993).
13. Alexandra Halkias, 'Democracy Revisited: Democracy and Agon in Modern Greece' (Ph.D. dissertation, University of California, San Diego, 1997); Heather Anne Paxson, 'Redefining Reproduction in Urban Greece: A Cultural Study of Fertility Control' (Ph.D. dissertation, Stanford University, 1998); idem, *Making Modern Mothers* (Berkeley, forthcoming).
14. See *Ours Once More*, pp.69, 108 ff.
15. George A. Megas, *The Greek House: Its Evolution and Its Relation to the Houses of the Other Balkan Peoples* (Athens, 1951).
16. Michael Thompson, *Rubbish Theory: The Creation and Destruction of Value* (Oxford, 1979).
17. Michael Herzfeld, *A Place in History: Social and Monumental Time in a Cretan Town* (Princeton, 1991).

The Construction of National Time: The Making of the Modern Greek Historical Imagination

ANTONIS LIAKOS

I awoke with this marble head in my hands
which exhausts my elbows and I do not know where to set it down.
It was falling into the dream as I was coming out of the dream
our lives joined thus and it will be difficult to part them

George Seferis, *Mythical Story*

As modern history writing has developed since the nineteenth century, the concept of the nation has become one of the essential categories for the construction of notions of space and time.[1] This is the tradition and the institutional environment within which contemporary historians conduct their research and write their texts, reconstructing and reinforcing the structures of power that they experience.

The concept of the nation has been approached from two basically different perspectives. The first concerns representations of national revival: the nation, a preexisting entity, resurrected and, under certain conditions, assumes an active historical role. The second perspective refers to interpretations of the construction of the nation through national ideology and the institutions of the political community. Theories of the first category (essentialist theories) are part of the national ideology, especially in its romantic and historicist phases. They refer to and eventually rationalize the way the nation perceives itself; more precisely, they describe the dominant view of the national ideology. Essentialist theories contribute to the construction of the nation. Since they have been transformed into ideology and acquired significance in space and time, in culture, and in institutions, they do not simply describe a process but reproduce their object. They constitute the reflection through which the nation constructs its self-image. As a result, they intervene in the processes of redefinition and construction of identities.[2] Theories of the second category (constructing theories), closer to the French tradition that conceptualizes the nation on the premise of a sense of belonging, have been shaped by the work of Frederik Barth, Eric

Hobsbawm and Terence Ranger, Benedict Anderson, Ernest Gellner, and others.[3] This theoretical framework has been enriched by post-1970s studies on ideology and the discursive construction of identities and now constitutes the common background of working theories of the nation within the international academic community.[4] These two approaches to the nation differ in their readings of the direction of time. In representation the direction is from the past to the present; in interpretation it is from the present to the past. Both directions relate to the reading of dreams. During dreaming, 'the preceding events are caused by the ending, even if, in narrative composition as we know it, the ending is linked to the events which precede it by a cause and effect relationship'.[5] This is also the time of history making. History and national ideology share the double time of the dream. As Seferis wrote, 'it was falling into the dream as I was coming out of the dream'.

TIME AND THE NATIONAL NARRATIVE

National identity, having a temporal structure, imposes a restructuring of the perception of time. This perception is articulated as narrative; it is formulated in the shape of national history using the organic category of the nation. The national narrative identifies subjects with the national collectivity and represents the nation; it consolidates these identifications in the domains of institutions and of symbols; it influences, clarifies, and unifies different traditions, thus constructing a national culture. The construction of the national narrative restructures the experience of time, attributing new significance to it and presenting the nation as an active historical agent that, through the narrative, acquires a new historical identity.[6] In this sense, national historiography constitutes a codified past which is revived through present action aimed at an expected future. In other words, it embodies a significant and ever-present element of the nation, its active memory. Memory, however, since it has been activated and articulated in a certain narrative, cannot accept gaps. This means that a national narrative should have internal coherence and no temporal discontinuities. The question of continuity has acquired crucial importance in the construction of national history, particularly for Mediterranean nations.

MEDITERRANEAN PARTS

The Mediterranean nations have awakened with a marble head in their hands. The need to deal with long historical periods and diverse cultures is a common feature of their national histories. They have undertaken the difficult task of combining different significant pasts – synthesizing the Greek–Roman world with the Christian, the Latin with the German, the Greek with the Slav and the Ottoman world, the Egyptian, the Hellenistic, the Roman, the Islamic, the Arab, the Ottoman past, colonialism and independence. These pasts have various meanings for the construction of Mediterranean identities and the shaping of national cultures and politics.

How, for instance, should the Christian nations' *historia sacra* and *historia profana* be made compatible, or the Arab, Iranian, and Ottoman be reconciled with the Islamic past? Is the Hellenistic period part of the history of Egypt, or does it belong to the history of Greece? To whose history does Byzantium belong? Is it Greek, or does it belong equally to Bulgaria and Serbia? Is the Ottoman period an integrated part of Balkan and Arab history or a foreign interruption of it? Does Macedonian history belong to a Southern Slav, a Hellenic, or a local Macedonian tradition? Is the history of early modern Thessaloniki part of a history of the Jewish Diaspora, Ottoman history, or Greek history? Is there a place in the Balkan national histories for non-national, ethnic and religious minorities such as the Sephardic Jews, the Vlachs, the Greek Catholics, and the Turkish-speaking Orthodox populations? All these questions relate to identities. Is Egyptian identity Arab, Islamic, or geographic and cultural (child of the Nile)? What are the consequences for domestic or foreign policy of the adoption of one or another of these definitions of identity?[7]

THE PRODUCTION OF TIME

The appropriation and the resignification of these pasts involve the adjustment of different perceptions of the structure of time.[8] Consequently, the homogenization of the way people perceive time is a necessary precondition for the construction of national historical time. The narration of this national time implies the incorporation of temporal units into a coherent scheme. This process is particularly depicted in historiography and the philosophy of history. The construction of historical time is conducted in stages and with hesitations and contradictions. What it involves is not simply the appropriation of a part of historical experience but the construction in the present of a discourse that reproduces the past and transforms it into national time. In other words, it is a process of the production of time. According to Paul Ricoeur, history in its narrative form replaces the history which has been collectively experienced,[9] constructing the basic myth of the nation. The rearrangement of the collective sense of time is a presupposition of the construction of the nation, and at the same time the nation constructs a collective sense of time.

THE GREEK CASE

Revivalism

Greek historiography is a product of the Greek national state. During the foundation of the new state the constitutive myth was the resurrection of the mythical Phoenix.[10] Its significance was that Greece had been resurrected after having been successfully subjugated by the Macedonians, the Romans, the Byzantines, and the Turks. The first rector of the University of Athens, Constantine Schinas, referred to the metaphor of an enslaved Greece handed over by the Macedonians to the Romans and then by the Byzantines to the Turks.[11] This was the first official view of Greek history in the aftermath of the war of liberation in 1821. As a consequence, the first period to become part of the national sense of history was that of classical antiquity. The appropriation of this period was accomplished under the influence of the Enlightenment, about 50 years before the Greek revolution and despite the reservations on the part of the post-Byzantine Orthodox Church.[12] The myth of ancient Greece was also powerful outside the Greek-speaking society of the Ottoman empire. The modern Greeks used it to introduce themselves to other nations, although it is an oversimplification to consider Greek identity simply a product of post-Enlightenment colonialism.[13]

The story of the incorporation of the myth of ancient Greece into the national ideology is complex and controversial. The most powerful tradition, even before the creation of nation-states, was that of written texts, Greek, Latin, and Hebrew.[14] This written tradition was the corpus from which prenational history was shaped, and before the emergence of nation-states myths of national origins were connected to this written tradition.[15] Greeks appropriated much of this learned tradition and transformed it into a national tradition. This appropriation was not an isolated case. Hellenism as a cultural topos was an intellectual product of the Renaissance revived by intellectual trends ranging from the Enlightenment to Romanticism.[16] As concepts, Hellenism and revival were closely linked. The Renaissance having introduced a threefold conception of time (ancient, medieval, and modern), revivalism was established as the intellectual model, and every major change in culture until Romanticism was presented as a revival.[17] Indeed, nationalism can be defined, in this framework, as 'myths of the historical renovation'.[18] The first incorporation, as a result, constitutes not simply the beginning of the national narrative but actually the construction of the object of this narrative. For Greeks, feeling like a nation means internalizing their relationship with ancient Greece.

Another aspect which should not be underestimated is that the revival of antiquity was not aimed exclusively at the legitimation of genealogy. Classical antiquity was also projected as the ideal model for the organization of a modern society. One of the most important works of early modern Greek historiography, George Kozakis Tipaldos's 1839 *Philosophical Essay on the Progress and Decline of Ancient Greece*, reflects this attitude.[19] The exemplary and nomothetic function of the ancient world is not limited to the construction of the modern Greek state but part of a transcultural tradition. This important role of the other (that is, the ancient) world, deeply embedded in historical consciousness, has to do with notions of authority, power, sacredness, and truth. Thus concepts of the world originate from another world in the remote past. To this same tradition could be ascribed the uses of the Torah for Israel and of the Koran and the Shariah for the Muslim nations.[20]

Continuity

During the first decades of Greek independence, the initial present–past relationship had two poles: the national resurrection (the 1821 revolution and the formation of the Greek state) and classical antiquity. The myth of the phoenix, however, was too weak to sustain a national ideology, especially since it involved an immense time gap. Moreover, it excluded an important part of the present religious experience.[21] The blank pages of Greek history became visible in the middle of the nineteenth century. The historian Spyridon Zambelios wrote in 1852: 'We only hope that all those scattered and torn pieces of our history will be articulated and succeeded by completeness and unity.'[22] Filling these gaps meant supplying criteria for the appropriation of periods such as the Macedonian domination of Greece, the Hellenistic and Roman period, the Byzantine era, and periods of Venetian and Ottoman rule. In 1872 the philosopher Petros Vrailas Armenis referred briefly to the meanings that should be stressed for each period: [23]

> With regard to the historical past of Greece, meaning the mission of Hellenism, it is necessary to examine the ways in which Greece is related to its preceding Oriental world, what it was, the influence it exercised on the Romans, its relation to Christianity, what happened to Greece in the Middle Ages, how Greece contributed to the Renaissance, how it contributes to contemporary civilization, how and why it has survived to this day despite its enslavement, and how it has resurrected itself, which is its mission today.

In this view, history is identified with the nation's mission and, as a consequence, it is Divine Providence that attributes meaning to it. The incorporation also refers to the nation's relation to the surrounding world. In other words, it constitutes a national reading of world history. This is, however, a particular 'world history' concentrated on Western European civilization, recognized as its peak – a reading of world history from a

Eurocentric point of view. In fact, this perspective lays the foundation for a dialectic between European and Greek national historiography. On the one hand, it aims at the emancipation of national history from Eurocentrism (contempt of Byzantium as a degeneration of the Roman empire) while, on the other, it evaluates national history for its contribution to European history, that is, the history of Western civilization.

The filling of these gaps was the task of historiography during the second half of the nineteenth century. In 1918 the historian Spyridon Lambros, summarizing the historical production of the first century of the independent Greek state, pointed out that 'a coherent conception of Greek history, representing the fortune of a people maintaining its existence and consciousness throughout the ages, emerged very late'.[24] The incorporation into the national narrative of the various periods that would contribute to the making of national history took place in stages and not without debate.

The timing of each incorporation involved a relationship between Greek and Western European historiography. For example, the appropriation of the Macedonian and the Hellenistic periods was facilitated by the concept of national supremacy. Within the debate in nineteenth century German historiography on the reassessment of the Hellenistic period, it became possible to present Hellenism (with the meaning and the cultural characteristics that were attributed to it at the time) as the predecessor of Christianity and to establish an imperial ideal (especially in the works of Johann Gustav Droysen).[25] However, the contempt for Byzantium of Voltaire, Gibbon, and Hegel – in other words, the negative attitude that developed towards it within the framework of the Enlightenment – prevented its incorporation at this stage.[26] Moreover, since the concept of 'Hellenism' as a cultural construction of western civilization was restricted by philhellenes to the revival of modern Greece, the rejection of Byzantium along with all the other historical periods between the classical age and the Greek revolt in 1821 was unavoidable. To span the huge gap between the classical ideal and the reality of modern Greece, the concept of a decline and fall was inevitable: Byron, in *Childe Harold's Pilgrimage* (canto 2, stanza 73), called the modern Greeks a 'sad relic of departed worth'. Otherwise, the concept of revival itself would have contained a discontinuity, and a national narrative could not entertain discontinuity.

The appropriation of the Byzantine period is of major significance because it represents the transition from one structure of the historical imagination to another: from the schema of revival to one of continuity. This transition is primarily a matter of the concept of historical time. Once this transition has been accomplished, each historical period finds its place within this schema. The result of this change was Constantinos Paparrigopoulos's monumental *History of the Greek Nation (1860–1874).*

Paparrigopoulos, honoured as 'national historian', created the grand narrative and introduced a new style to national historiography.[27] Although his predecessors had employed the third person in referring to their object, Paparrigopoulos imposed a very dominant use of 'we' and 'us' in describing the Greeks of the past, thus identifying the reader with the national subject. In addition, the appropriation of Byzantine history turned the national identity into a native-produced one. This change acquired the features of a revolt against the national self-image that had been imposed on Greece by European classicism. It was a response to a general feeling of nineteenth century Greek intellectuals: 'The Past? Alas, we allow foreigners to present it according to their own prejudices and to their own way of thinking and interests.'[28]

Inside and Outside Western Europe

At the same time, of course, the agents of the incorporation of Byzantium into the national history attempted to define the contribution of Byzantium to Western civilization. This became another permanent feature of Greek historical culture: keeping Greek national history beyond the influence of Western historical thinking, on the one hand, and, on the other hand, considering it an essential contribution to Western culture – both resisting the western canon of history and participating in it. For example, the present archbishop of the Greek Orthodox Church insists that Greeks should not learn Byzantine history from foreigners and that Byzantine history is one of the foundations of contemporary European identity. This attitude might be compared with modern Islamic attitudes towards history: '[Islamic history] is influenced by Western education, [which is unable] to understand Islam … The mind that will judge Islamic life must be Islamic in its essence.'[29] Attempting to construct a grammar of such attitudes would be one approach to the relational structure of national historiographies. From a non-Western point of view, there is a move from the suppression of entire past periods located outside the Western cultural tradition to the idealization of these same periods as distinctive cultural features and as contributions to world civilization. Another Mediterranean example of this oscillation is the case of Turkish historiography of the Ottoman period. Suppressed during the Ataturk era, the Ottoman empire has come to be considered the solution to the peasant problem and a third way between capitalism and socialism.[30]

This move from outside definitions of national history and identity to their self-definition and from intellectual elites to ordinary people is an attempt to relocate the centre of national history: 'While ordinary people recognize that it is to the medieval period that they owe their existence, their language, and their religion, it is only intellectuals who deny it.'[31] This is another oscillation between the claims of history to scientific status, on the one hand and the mistrust of intellectuals writing history, on the other.

Appropriation of a past culture is a long process. Thus, a lengthy period of time passed between the legitimation of Byzantium as part of the national narrative and historians' use of it in national symbolism and representation. Byzantium was not reassessed in textbooks until the end of the nineteenth century; the Byzantine Museum was not established until 1914, and the first professors of Byzantine art and history were appointed at the University of Athens only in 1912 and 1924 respectively.[32] Appropriation takes place in stages with regard not only to the concrete setting of the specific period but also to its various aspects. Thus the theory of the unity of Greek history has been transferred from political history to linguistics[33] and folklore.[34] In the case of Byzantium, this process took several decades to complete, and new images are still in play. The delay in the development of Byzantine studies in Western Europe emphasizes the fact that international historical debate may affect national history but does not entirely determine it.

National Geneology

The construction of the 'unity' of Greek history also created its narrative form. The innovation in Paparrigopulos's work lies in the fact that it reifies Greek history and organizes it in terms of a main characteristic giving a particular meaning to each period. His first Hellenism is 'Ancient Hellenism', the classical Hellenism that declined after the Peloponnesian Wars. It is succeeded by 'Macedonian Hellenism', actually 'a slight transformation of the first Hellenism'. This is followed by 'Christian Hellenism', which is later replaced by the 'medieval Hellenism' from which 'modern Hellenism' emerges in the thirteenth century. A genealogy connects these Hellenisms:

Ancient Hellenism	father	great-great-grandfather
Macedonian Hellenism	son	great-grandfather
Christian Hellenism	grandson	grandfather
Medieval Hellenism	great-grandson	father
Modern Hellenism	great-great-grandson	son

The specific features that differentiate or, rather, give substance to each Hellenism, are formed according to the 'historical order' prescribed by Divine Providence, in other words, its 'mission' or 'final aim'. These orders are related to the nation's past or expected future contribution to world history.

The crucial question is the relation of these Hellenisms to the nation. An exploration of the internal logic is not helpful here. On the contrary, if we approach the question from a morphological point of view, we soon realize that it is actually a transfer to history of the religious concept of the Holy Trinity – the same essence in multiple expressions. The schema ultimately has a theological point of reference which became obvious in Droysen's use of the term 'Hellenism', although Paparrigopoulos used it differently.[35] The idea has been transformed and diffused. A century later, the Marxist historian Nikolaos Svoronos would face the same problem: 'Hellenism as a metaphysical entity, as a *sui generis* genre, does not participate in changes in the environment, and as a result it remains continuous, coherent and unchanging in its qualities'.[36] National historiography, even in its Marxist version, remained founded on metaphysics.

The conceptual construct of multiple Hellenisms solves various problems that were intractable both for the theory of revival and for the theory of continuity because the narrative structure of Hellenisms is one of unity through difference. The revival survives within the schema of continuation. In Paparrigopoulos's work, the rise of modern Hellenism in the thirteenth century is related to the rediscovery of ancient Hellenism: 'The fall of Constantinople [to the Crusaders in 1204] reorientes our minds and hearts towards historical Athens'. It is ancient Hellenism that provides modern Hellenism its political component and makes national independence possible without the intervention of Europe and the impact of the Renaissance and the Enlightenment. Thus the revival becomes a radical political identity. The historical argument here is that national consciousness was the result of the elaboration of political consciousness through its relation to the civic culture of classical Greece.

Nevertheless, the incongruity between Hellenism and the Greek nation has survived to this day. That references to 'Hellenism' outnumber references to 'the Greek Nation' in contemporary historical culture conceals a contempt of the political process by which the Greek nation has been constituted and the downgrading of citizenship to the status of an ethnonationalistic definition of Greek identity. In this way Greek identity has been purified of 'alien' elements, most obviously in the politics of and popular attitudes towards minorities in Greece, and through the elaboration of the term 'Hellenism' an ethnocultural definition of the nation has been imposed.

Cultural History

The norton of different Hellenisms created a problem for the historical appropriation of the periods since the disintegration of the Byzantine empire in 1204. The period of the Frankish occupation was combined with the Byzantine period, but it was also connected with the period of the Venetian occupation, in its turn interwoven with that of Ottoman rule. New axes were necessary for the incorporation of this field into the national narrative, and new meanings needed to be attributed to it. Greek historiography, without the backbone of political history, used cultural history as a substitute.

The first approach, which originated in Western and more precisely in Renaissance historiography, was through the contribution of Byzantine scholars to Italian humanism in the fourteenth and fifteenth centuries, which extended to the myth that the Greeks were responsible for the revival of civilization in modern Europe.[37] This powerful myth largely influenced the formation of the Greek national myth, the Great Idea. 'Greece is destined to enlighten the West with its decline and the East with its resurrection'.[38] It was to be expected, of course, that this particular perception, stressing the nation's contribution to world history, would be pointed to not only as a chance event but more or less from the perspective of 'The History of Greek education from the fall of Constantinople till 1821'.[39] Since education was an indication of progress, it was obvious that the history of the progress of the nation would emphasize the history of the expansion of education. Interest in scholars who had promoted interaction between Byzantium and the West had already been introduced by Andreas Moustoxidis and his periodical *Hellinomnimon* (1843–47).[40] The origins of modern Hellenism were pursued in the history of literature and erudition. Research was mainly oriented towards the vernacular texts of the last centuries of the Byzantine empire, with emphasis on literature and culture in Crete during the five centuries of Venetian rule. Scholars therefore turned to the Venetian archives, which provided new ground for Greek historiography.[41] In order to be incorporated into the national narrative, the history of the Venetian period was adapted to the demands of national ideology. 'In an a posteriori judgement, one would say that this mastery of Hellenism by Western peoples has proved fateful ever since. Because of the interaction of the two elements [Greek and Latin], the revival of art and scholarship became possible in the West'.[42]

The most conspicuous effort was the exploration of the characteristics of the Hellenic 'soul' in Cretan literature and painting and the emergence of the idea of a Greek Renaissance through Cretan culture.[43] Thus cultural history filled the gap created by the lack of political supremacy of the nation. It is interesting in this regard that cultural history, dealing with the biographies of literary men and literature, and not political history has been the traditional genre of modern Greek historiography.

The Ottoman Legacy

A great problem for Greek historiography was the appropriation of the four centuries of Ottoman rule from 1453 until 1821, called the Turkokratia (Turkish occupation). With this term, four centuries are detached from a longer period of the Ottoman presence in the northeastern Mediterranean, dating from the eleventh century to the second decade of the twentieth century. For nineteenth century Greek society, this period was its immediate past, still alive in its everyday culture, although the cultural debate had been suppressed as a cause of Greece's backwardness. At the same time it was mythologized as the cradle of national virtues. In historiography the Turkokratia was considered as a passive period of slavery and at the same time as having procedure, in the words of Paparrigopoulos, 'the military, bourgeois, and intellectual forces that realized the Greek revolution'. The history of this period was mixed with historical mythology seeking to justify the ideological, social, and political balance of power in postrevolutionary Greece. It should be pointed out that each historical period was appropriated through a different discourse. Whereas the canon of Greek history was defined by Paparrigopoulos, the epistemological rupture in neohellenic historiography is related to Lambros's importation of historical positivism.[44] This rupture was not just a matter of the establishment of a positivistic discourse. While the nation had been convinced that all preceding historical periods belonged to it, the new social and further cultural demands of the twentieth century called for a different knowledge of this recent past.

Demoticism and Socialism

One of the most important intellectual movements at the end of nineteenth and the beginning of the twentieth century was demoticism, the movement for the adoption of the vernacular as the official language. Demoticism proposed the term 'Romiosyni' instead of 'Hellenism' for Greek identity. The term disassociated modern Greek identity from the classical past and adopted a more diffuse, popular, and immediate feeling for identity, that of Romaioi, the self-nomination of Greeks during the Byzantine and Ottoman centuries. However, demoticism's perception of the national past was no different from the official one; it basically aimed at the transformation of the discourse of national identity through literature and linguistic change. In spite of this, the demoticists were accused of attempting to disrupt the unity of national history, and in response they emphasized sociology rather than history. However, they did manage to graft onto the hegemonic version of Greek continuity a strong (and positive) sensitivity towards the nation's recent past and particularly towards the cultural tradition of recent periods.[45]

The hegemonic version of history went unchallenged even by the socialists and the Marxists. They did, however, challenge the prevailing version of the Greek revolution, mainly through the work of George Skliros (*Our Social Question*, 1908) and Yannis Kordatos (*The Social Significance of the Revolution of 1821*, 1924), and thus provoked an intense political debate on the origins of the revolution and its agency. This debate was the result of a reorientation of Greek intellectuals' interest from the unification of the nation towards the 'social question' under the influence of the socialist revolution in Russia and the emergence of the Greek socialist movement.[46] The influx of Greek populations from Asia Minor and the Balkans into Greece in 1922 and the social crisis of the interwar years and World War II, including the Resistance and the Civil War, posed the question of the redefinition of national identity. Thus the first serious works on Greek society during Ottoman rule were those of Michael Sakellariou,[47] Apostolos Vakalopoulos,[48] Nikos Svoronos,[49] and Costantinos Dimaras,[50] which paved the way for a new approach to the Turkokratia and the establishment modern Greek historiography in the years during and after World War II.

To be effective, the appropriation of the Turkokratia needed an interpretive narrative. This was offered by Dimaras, who introduced the term 'Neohellenic Enlightenment' to historical discourse in 1945. Through this term, all the events of the Turkokratia were viewed from a different perspective. Dimaras introduced a new organization of time, a new discourse, and new research priorities that meant a shift in the paradigm relating to the period. Through this schema, Hellenism assumed an active role in the period of Ottoman rule and the historical narrative gained coherence and orientation. Thus, a 'missing' period was integrated into national time. The national narrative composed by Paparrigopoulos was concluded by the Dimaras narrative but this conclusion had a paradoxical effect. In his writings, Dimaras had revived the debate on the issue of national identity, offering alternative suggestions and new concepts that came from Western Europe with regard to the construction of the nation. Emphasizing the role of intellectuals, the development of their communicative networks, and their social mobility, he managed to reveal the processes and constituent elements of nation building and its self-consciousness. In this way, he deconstructed the prevailing representations of the nation even though he himself was unfamiliar with interpretive theories of the nation. At the same time, however, he did not deconstruct the broader schema of national time that Paparrigopoulos has created.

In addition to Dimaras, another strong influence on studies of the Turkokratia came from the work of Nikos Svoronos. He emphasized the economic and social history of the period and particularly the emergence of a class with modern economic activities. This thematic shift reoriented historical studies from the political and cultural events of the revolution to the social realities of the period which preceded it. However, Svoronos's influence on the wider public is chiefly due to his *History of Modern Greece*.[51] If in the Enlightenment School the schema of history was the modernist elite versus the inert masses, the schema of Marxist history advocated by Svoronos was society and the people versus the 'state' and the mechanisms of local and foreign power.

History and Aesthetics

The literature of the modernist 'Generation of the '30s', the interest in popular art (Angeliki Hatzimihali), and the transformation of the aesthetic canon in the interwar period (Dimitris Pikionis, Fotis Kontoglou) had provided the broader cultural framework within which a new reading of the history of the Turkokratia became possible. It was the period of the Resistance to the German occupation that revived the references to the Revolution of 1821 and created historical analogies. Thus, the historical appropriation of the period of Ottoman rule came in the twentieth century and brought with it the late study of modern Greek history and its isolation from the Ottoman and Balkan context. The first professor of modern Greek history at the University of Athens was appointed as late as 1937.

Through these experiences came, first, a popular reading of the hegemonic version of history and, secondly, a connection between history and aesthetics. The popular reading of history was as a plot in which the Greek people were the victims of foreign intervention and popular efforts at progress were frustrated by imposed regimes. The Marxist and anti-imperialist spirit of the time is obvious in this reading. The connection between history and aesthetics meant the historicization of aesthetics and the aestheticization of history. The discourses during the interwar years about '*Hellinikotita*' (the equivalent of *Hispanidad* or *Italianità*) resulted in a search for authenticity in the tradition and contributed to a consideration of history as part of the aesthetic canon, from high cultural activities to popular entertainment.[52] The modernist poetry of Yannis Ritsos, George Seferis, and Odisseas Elitis and the popularization of poetry through the music of Mikis Theodorakis and Manos Hatzidakis in the postwar period spread this sentimental affection for national history. This popular reading of history, enriched by aesthetics, emerged with the end of the dictatorship in 1974, and in the 1980s there was a renewed attachment to a national history politicized by the socialists of Andreas Papandreou: 'Greece for the Greeks.' When the socialist ideals sank after 1989, what remained was the popular attachment to the great historical continuities, Hellenism and Orthodoxy. With the disappearance of anti-imperialism, a kind of nativism with anti-Western colours surfaced. It is therefore no surprise that when the 'Macedonian crisis' exploded in 1991–93 this attachment to history prevailed over all other political considerations. Politicians had argued like historians; history, even without historians, had become a decisive force for determining politics.[53]

The Modernization of National History

The modernization of national history coincided with an attempt at the revival of neohellenic historiography. However, the postwar period was not favourable for the development of research. Even the suspicion that historical work disputed the official version of history was enough to incur legal consequences for the author. Thus, when Svoronos published his history in Paris in 1955, he was deprived of his passport. It took more than 20 years after the end of the war for modern Greek history to be incorporated into the national narrative. In the past 20 years, the majority of Greek historians have been influenced by the French *Annales* school, with a tinge of Western Marxism, by British and American social science, and, more or less, by the school of the history of the Greek Enlightenment created by Dimaras. The traditional history of the nation has been replaced by a new history of the society, creating a critical counterbalance to the pressure of nationalism. Criticism of the national ideology and representations, the construction of the national narrative and identity, and the history of the Greek minorities emerged in the 1990s as new topics in Greek historiography. Yet despite what is happening within the community of historians, the structure of national time elaborated over the past two centuries persists in the public use of history and in historical culture. The marble head that tires our arms is difficult to set down.

NOTES

1. James Sheeham, 'What is German History? Reflections on the Role of the "Nation" in German History and Historiography', *Journal of Modern History*, 53 (1981), pp.1–23.
2. Anthony Smith, *Theories of Nationalism* (London, 1983).
3. Frederik Barth, *Ethnic Groups and Boundaries* (London, 1969); Eric Hobsbawm and Terence Ranger, *The Invention of Tradition* (Cambridge, 1983); Benedict Anderson, *Imagined Communities* (London, 1983); Ernest Gellner, *Nations and Nationalism* (Oxford, 1983).
4. For an assessment of this transition from essentialist to constructivist theories of the nation, see Cora Govers and Hans Vermeulen (eds.), *The Politics of Ethnic Consciousness* (London, 1977), pp.1–30.
5. Boris A. Uspenskij, *Storia e semiotica* (Milan, 1988), p.13.
6. On the restructuring of the experience of time through narrative, see Paul Ricoeur, *Time and Narrative* (Chicago, 1983), pp.52–87, and on the term 'appropriation of the past', see his *Mémoire, oubli et histoire* (Florence, 1995).
7. Jack Crabbs, *The Writing of History in Nineteenth-Century Egypt* (Cairo, 1984); Anthony Gorman, 'In the Shadow of the Nation: The Politics of Egyptian Historiography in the Twentieth Century', *Journal of Arabic, Islamic, and Middle Eastern Studies*, 3 (1996), pp.117–26; Israel Gershoni, 'Imagining and Reimagining the Past: The Use of History by Egyptian Nationalist Writers, 1919–1952', *History and Memory*, 4 (1992), pp.6–37; David Gordon, 'History and Identity in Arab Textbooks', *Princeton Near East Papers*, 13 (1971), pp.1–15.
8. Reinhart Koselleck, *Futures, Pasts: On the Semantics of Historical Time* (Boston, 1985).
9. Ricoeur, *Time and Narrative*, pp.52–87.

10. Loukia Droulia, 'Ta symvola tou neou ellinikou kratous', *Ta Istorika*, 23 (1995) pp.335–51.
11. K. Th. Dimaras, *En Athinais ti 3 Maiou 1837* (Athens, 1987), p.31.
12. Paschalis Kitromilidis, 'Imagined Communities and the Origins of the National Question in the Balkans', in Th. Veremis and M. Blichorn (eds.), *Modern Greece: Nationalism and Nationality* (Athens, 1990), pp.23–66.
13. Stathis Gourgouris, *Dream Nation: Enlightenment, Colonization, and the Institution of Modern Greece* (Stanford, 1996).
14. R.R. Bolgar, *The Classical Heritage and Its Beneficiaries* (Cambridge, 1973); U. von Wilamowitz-Moellendorf, *History of Classical Scholarship* (London, 1982); Vassilis Lambropoulos, *The Rise of Eurocentrism* (Princeton, 1992).
15. R.E. Asher, *National Myth in Renaissance France* (Edinburgh, 1993); Collette Beaune, *Naissance de la nation France* (Paris, 1985); Eugen Weber, *My France: Politics, Culture, Myth* (Cambridge, MA, 1991); Eoin Macneill, *Celtic Ireland* (Dublin, 1981); W.B. Stanford, *Ireland and the Classical Tradition* (Dublin, 1976).
16. Frank Turner, *The Greek Heritage in Victorian Britain* (New Haven, 1981); Olga Augustinos, *French Odysseys: Greek in French Travel Literature from the Renaissance to the Romantic Era* (Baltimore, 1994); Moses Hadas, *Humanism: The Greek Ideal and Its Survival* (New York, 1960); Suzanne Marchand, *Down from Olympus* (Princeton, 1996); Margarita Milioris, 'The Greek Nation in British Eyes 1821–1864: Aspects of a British Discourse on Nationality, Politics, History, and Europe' (Ph.D. Diss., Oxford University, 1998).
17. W.K. Ferguson, *The Renaissance in Historical Thought* (Cambridge, 1948); Peter Burke, *The Renaissance Sense of the Past* (New York, 1970).
18. Smith, *Theories of Nationalism*, p.22; Hutchinson John, *The Dynamics of Cultural Nationalism: The Gaelic Revival and the Creation of the Irish Nation-State* (London, 1987).
19. George Kozakis Tipaldos, *Filosofiko dokimio gia tin anodo kai tin ptosi tis palaias Ellados* (Athens, 1839).
20. V.N. Volossinov, *Marxism and the Philosophy of Language* (New York, 1973), Part 2, p.75. See also Peter van der Veer and Hartmut Lehman (eds.), *Nation and Religion* (Princeton, 1999); Yosef Hayim Yerushalmi, *Zakhor: Jewish History and Jewish Memory* (Washington, DC, 1982); Yael Zerubavel, *Recovered Roots: Collective Memory and the Making of Israeli National Tradition* (Chicago, 1995).
21. Elli Skopetea, *To 'protypo vasileio' kai I Megali Idea* (Athens, 1988).
22. Spyridon Zambelios, *Dimotika asmata tis Ellados* (Corfu, 1852), p.16.
23. Petros Vrailas Armenis, *Peri tis istorikis apostolis tis Ellados* (Corfu, 1872), p.4.
24. Spyridon Lambros, 'Historical Studies in Greece during the First Century of Independence with an Introduction about Greek Historical Writing during the Period of Ottoman Rule' (manuscript, University of Athens, 1918), Ch. 7, pp.1–2.
25. Arnaldo Momigliano, 'J.G. Droysen tra Greci ed Ebrei', in *Tra Storia e Storicismo* (Pisa, 1985), pp.211–35.
26. Dionysios Zakythinos, 'Le monde de Byzance dans la pensée historique de l'Europe a partir du XVIIe siècle', in *Byzance: Etat-société-économie* (London, 1973), pp.41–96.
27. K.Th. Dimaras, *Constantinos Paparrigopoulos* (Athens, 1986).
28. Zambelios, *Dimotika asmata*, p.7.
29. Yvonne Yarbeck Haddad, *Contemporary Islam and the Challenge of History* (New York, 1980), p.166.
30. Halil Berktay, 'The Search for the Peasant in Western and Turkish History/Historiography', in H. Berktay and Suraiya Faroqhi, *New Approaches to State and Peasant in Ottoman History* (London, 1992), p.156.
31. C. Paparrigopoulos, Preface to the Vols. 3 and 4 of the *History of the Greek Nation* (Athens, 1885–88).
32. Christina Koulouri, *Dimensions idéologiques de l' historicité en Grece (1834–1914)* (Frankfurt am Main, 1991); Tonia Kiousopoulou, 'I proti edra Byzantinis Istorias sto Panepistimio Athinon', *Mnimon*, 15 (1993), pp.257–76.
33. Georgios Hatzidakis, *Syntomos istoria tis ellinikis glossis* (Athens, 1915).
34. Nikolaos Politis, *Meleti epi tou viou ton neoteron Ellinon: Neoelliniki Mythologia* (Athens, 1871).

35. This idea is expressed in a text titled 'Theologie der Geschichte' with which he prefaced the 1843 edition of the *Geschichte des Hellenismus*. The relationship between theology and history is implemented in the development of history itself, of which the philosophy of history constitutes a transitional phase. The philosophy of history, of course, contributes to the secularization of history but is entirely related to religious perceptions.
36. Nikos Svoronos, 'Reflections on an Introduction in Neohellenic History', in *Analekta Neoellinikis Istorias kai Istoriographias* (Athens, 1982), p.71.
37. Deno Geanakoplos, *Greek Scholars in Venice* (Harvard, 1962); N.G. Wilson, *From Byzantium to Italy: Greek Studies in the Italian Renaissance* (London, 1992).
38. In this metaphor, used by Prime Minister Ioannis Koletis in 1844, Greece is like a candle. With the fall of the Byzantine empire, the light migrated to the West, but with the national revolution of 1821 the candle was destined to illuminate the East. K.Th. Dimaras, *Romantismos* (Athens, 1982), pp.405–7.
39. This was the title of the fourth Rodokanakeios Literary Competition in 1865, in which Constantinos Sathas was awarded the first prize for his work *Neoelliniki philologia: Biographiai ton en tois grammasi dialampsanton Ellinon apo tis kataliseos tis Vizantinis Aftokratorias mehri tis Ellinikis Ethnegersias (1453–1821)* (Athens, 1868).
40. Andreas Moustoxidis was an intellectual from Corfu who attempted to connect Italian to Ionian scholarship. His work belongs partly to Italian literature.
41. M. Manousakas, 'Syntomos episkopisis ton peri tin Venetokratopumenin Kritin erevnon', *Kritika Chronika*, 23 (1971), pp.245–308.
42. Spyridon Theotokis, *Eisagogi eis tin erevnan ton mnimeion tis istorias tou ellinismou kai idia tis Kritis en to kratiko archeio tou Venetikou kratous* (Corfu, 1926), p.3.
43. George Seferis, *Dokimes* (Athens, 1981), pp.268–319; David Holton (ed.), *Logotechnia kai koinonia stin Kriti tis Anagennisis* (Irakleio, 1997); Nikos Chatzinikolaou, 'Ethnikistikes diekdikiseis tou Dominikou Theotokopoulou', in José Alvarez Lopera (ed.), *El Greco: Tautotita kai Metamorfosi: Kriti, Italia, Ispania* (Milan, 1999), pp.61–87.
44. Effi Gazi, *Spyridon Lambros (1851–1919): 'Scientific' National History: The Greek Case in Comparative Perspective (1850–1920)* (Frankfurt am Main, 2000).
45. Dimitris Tziovas, *The Nationalism of the Demoticists and Its Impact on Their Literary Theory (1888–1930)* (Amsterdam, 1986).
46. George Dertilis, 'I istoriografia tou neoterou ellinismou simera', *Sygxrona Themata*, 36–7 (1988), pp.84–93.
47. Michael Sakellariou, *I Peloponnisos kata tin defteran Tourkokratia, 1715–1821* (Athens, 1939).
48. Apostolos Vakalopoulos, *Prosfiges kai Prosfigikon Zitima kata tin Ellinikin Epanastasin tou 1821* (Thessaloniki, 1939).
49. Nikos Svoronos, *Le commerce de Salonique au XVIIIe siècle* (Paris, 1956).
50. K.Th. Dimaras, *Istoria tis Neoellinikis Logotechnias* (Athens, 1945).
51. Nikos Svoronos, *Histoire de la Gréce moderne* (Paris, 1955); Greek edition, *Episkopisi tis Neoellinikis Istorias* (Athens, 1975).
52. Dimitris Tziovas, *Oi metamorfoseis tou ethnismou kai to ideologima tis ellinikotitas sto mesopolemo* (Athens, 1989); Artemis Leontis, *Topographies of Hellenism: Mapping the Homeland* (Ithaca and London, 1995).
53. A. Liakos, 'La crise dans les Balkans et le nationalisme en Gréce', *Science(s) Politique(s)*, 2–3 (Paris, 1993), pp.179–93.

Shifting Boundaries, Clientalism and Balkan Identities

DRAGO ROKSANDIĆ

The fact that three distinctive continental realities confront each other in the Mediterranena area makes comparative research there very difficult. Mediterranean Europe, Mediterranean Asia, and Mediterranean Africa are of uneven relevance within their respective continental frameworks, and at each point on the Mediterrean coast there is a tradition of contacts of different kinds with the quasi-totality of the Mediterranean world. These traditions are not always understood and appreciated, and therefore it is not always realistic, in historiographical terms, to insist upon comparative approaches, much less upon a comparative history. Fernand Braudel established a new area of intellectual communication with his *The Mediterranean and the Mediterranean World*,[1] and it would be unjust not to recognize its positive impact. Nevertheless, there has been no new major intellectual breakthrough since. He himself, turning his attention to the world and to France, has not produced anything to match that initial work, and in his own country many of its components have been rejected.

The Mediterranean heritage has everywhere been internalized in a national 'grand narrative' and even critically reevaluated, but generally without meeting the challenge of a comparative Mediterranean interpretation. Too much concerned with an exceptionalist attitude towards their respective national heritages, historians in the Mediterranean area, although accepting the idea of shared Mediterranean roots, usually prefer to overlook what those involved in concrete historical terms. If they compare at all, they tend to insist upon differences. This obsession with differences can be treated not only to the imperatives of national historiographies functioning as national ideologies but to an earlier heritage of competiton among maritime cities, empires, religions, and so on. Although it may have been important at a particular point for a particular project of nation building in the Mediterranean area in the twentieth century, today it is usually perceived from outside as parochial, outdated, and susceptible to misuse. But this attitude towards differences in detail can be a way of 'deconstructing' each national 'grand narrative' and transforming it into an open field for a comparative history of the Mediterranean. Such a history could place all the components of the Mediterranean heritage in their appropriate historical context, either in micro or macro terms. Its 'differences' would be perceived not only in relation to the 'other' in modern terms but also as a principle for the reinterpretation of each particular national tradition, making it more complex, more 'Mediterranean', and even more humane, recognizable all over the Mediterranean world.

Historians must make comparisons to learn more both about the historical phenomena shared by distinctive Mediterranean heritages and about those that distinguishes them from one another. With very few exceptions, however, Mediterranean studies today are ethno-natiocentric, and this necessarily creates problems of historical perspective. The traditions of nation-states in the Mediterranean area may be deeply rooted, but they are a modern phenomenon, each being a controversial appropriation of a desired heritage that could usually be appropriated by someone else. This is not, of course, an argument against tacking any nation-state, national history, or historiography in the Mediterranean area as a unit of comparison within a certain defined context.

One has to accept, albeit reluctantly, that the units of comparison in the Mediterranean area should be nation-state. This reluctance stems from the recognition that the changing geopolitical realities of the twentieth century – changing boundaries, territories, and, in particular, populations within nation-states – make comparisons very difficult. It is impossible, however, to consider any aspect of these identities without starting with nation-states, in particular when one is dealing with the political uses of the past. The Mediterranean was a shared space of competing premodern identities long before the establishment of nation-states within it. Mediterranean nation-states have internalized this heritage of conflict in various ways to achieve control over the aspects of it that are relevant for nation building. Constant conflict over the past is one of the most embarrassing aspects of Mediterranean historiographies – along with central-eastern European ones. The problem is to 'dehistoricize' the nations of the Mediterranean – not, of course, by depriving them of their past but by placing their heritages in larger and, in particular, comparative contexts. This challenge has to be accepted from 'below' at the level of a national culture, but it cannot succeed without major regional, Mediterranean, and even broader intellectual and institutional support. Whether this can be expected of nations which are largely deprived of any real chance for a better future within a generation is another question.

THE BALKANS FROM A COMPARATIVE PERSPECTIVE

It is beyond any doubt that the Balkan countries of the nineteenth and twentieth centuries experienced a variety of very controversial problems with regard to their identities. In the first place, all of them are extremely heterogeneous in ethnic, linguistic, religious, and cultural terms, and none of these differences is based upon undisputed historical continuities within them. Constructing a national identity has always meant glorifying one aspect of the national legacy and marginalizing, neglecting, or even demonizing the others. In particular cases of ethnic, linguistic, and cultural similarities in traditional terms, nation building may have very serious conflicts among competing national ideologies. Contrary to widespread beliefs in the West, a shared religious identity does not necessarily make nations more tolerant of each other in terms of national ideologies and policy making, although nations which do not share a religious identity in the Balkans rather regularly 'justify' conflicts, when they emerge, in religious terms.

In the Balkan case, what is particularly important is that disputes and conflicts are rarely only internal. Although it is known elsewhere in the Mediterranean, this phenomena has recognizable Balkan aspects. Conflicts readily do include neighbouring countries and are often immediately 'internalized' by the adjacent neighbours because of ethnolinguistic, religious, or cultural considerations and interests. To sum up, these disputes have been almost continuous over the past two centuries, and the high level of interdependence across borders makes many of them almost insoluble in rational terms.

INTERNAL CONFLICTS OVER THE PAST AND THE FUTURE

All of the Balkan nations have striking internal, regional socioeconomic differences that partly coincide with ethnic, religious, or cultural divisions. These differences have been profoundly restructured in every Balkan country in the past 100 years because of shifts in the majority of the population from rural to urban areas. Furthermore, despite the important differences between Albania and Greece, and between Croatia and Bulgaria, both internal socioeconomic tensions and those among Balkan countries related to new sociodemographic realities are in a way phenomena of a 'redistribution of poverty'. This has become strikingly clear in the past decade, along with the collapse of 'real socialism' and the failure of any of these socioeconomic and sociocultural entities to transform themselves into viable modern nation-states. Balkan nations have rediscovered themselves as peripheral in many respects even in the Mediterranean context. This legacy has yet to be properly recognized by Balkan national ideologies and historiographies.

National ideologies and social sciences everywhere in the Balkans contain intellectual constructs about the 'uniqueness' of a particular national community. Although seemingly very different from each other, structurally they are very similar. They are primarily parochial – much more parochial than exceptionalist. This distinguishes the Balkans from other northern Mediterranean countries such as Italy and Spain, not to mention France.

EXTERNALIZATION OF INTERNAL CONFLICTS AND THEIR JUSTIFICATION

The major changes since 1989–91, after much national disillusionment, have confronted the majority of the Balkan countries with the prospect of peripheral status in Europe for decades to come. At the same time, the emerging political cultures dominating the region are to a large extent authoritarian in their roots, whether they pretend to be ideologically 'leftist' or 'rightist'. Such long-term peripheral status, combined with authoritarian political structures and cultures, 'predetermines' long-lasting internal tensions and even a lack of capacity to settle complex external problems in an internationally reliable way. This means that regional stability depends heavily upon extraregional intervention. This intervention, in turn, being obsessed with security considerations in larger geostrategical frameworks, unavoidably becomes part of the internal Balkan problem because of its tendency to include violence, the use of force and internationally justified extraparliamentary authority. Here again the Balkans differ from the other northern Mediterranean countries. Since it is often reminiscent of historical experiences in the Balkans, this situation can easily encourage those 'below' to relying upon geostrategical justifications of their particular self-perceptions and interests.

LACK OF IDENTITY AND THE POWER OF CLIENTELISM

Although it is not publicly acknowledged there, it is popularly believed that the Balkans cannot be a region in European terms. Securing one's future in such an area requires someone powerful enough outside it to protect and/or support one's national 'cause'. Because the Balkans have, since antiquity, been a meeting place of various competing imperial interests, there is a deep conviction throughout the region that one must assert the 'right' to enjoy 'imperial' protection in terms of exceptional aspects of one's own national identity in opposition to neighbouring ones. One nation has to be a more reliable client than others in the area in order to fulfil 'imperial' expectations either in civilizational or in cultural and/or religious terms. This is why almost every nation in southeastern Europe is represented in its self-perception and national myth as the bulwark of a particular universal system of values (Christianity, Islam, and so on). Since all the empires that dominated the Balkans in the past established military frontier systems, beginning with the Roman *limes* and going on to those established by the Habsburgs, the Venetians, and the Ottomans, not to mention the cold war's shifting boundaries in the Balkans, such clientelism can easily be projected onto the mainstream tendencies of European history from particular points of view in the Balkans. The problem is that such 'legitimation' is quite often controversial when it has to do with major religious and cultural traditions. Nowhere in Europe does Eastern Christianity extend as far west as in southeastern Europe, along with Islam, and almost nowhere in Europe does Western Christianity extend as far east. Shifting imperial boundaries in the past often transferred numerous communities from one side to the other, mixing them with or opposing them to others. This means that any attempt to establish a new *limes* of any kind today includes the risk of provoking a 'cleansing' of certain territories of 'unreliable' communities and, of course, especially individuals. This is what we have been witnessing for the past ten years. Without clientelistic self-justifications (or justifications) it would not have been possible for such a disaster to take place.

BALKAN EXCEPTIONALISM IN EUROPE

National exceptionalism in the Balkans is to a large extent also justified by the fact that ethnically and socioculturally the Balkans are really an exception in the northern Mediterranean. In contrast to the other two peninsular regions of the northern Mediterranean, which were profoundly Romanized in antiquity, the Balkans were only partially so. The only Slavs to have reached the Mediterranean are settled in the Balkans, establishing in a way continuities with the Illyrians and the Thracians. Almost nowhere in the northern Mediterranean is there a nation like Albania, which preserves pre-Slavic continuities but escaped any effective integration into the ancient civilizations – not to mention the Hungarians and Bulgarians, to the extent that they are of Asian origin. Bearing in mind the importance of *Blut* and *Boden* in national myth and ideology making, such a variety of legacies, intermediated by different later imperial ones and different monotheistic religions, produces an almost incomprehensible multitude of types of national discourse in exceptionalist and exclusivist terms.

Such experiences facilitate the emergence of national myths and ideologies that are always ready to justify intolerance towards the 'other' and violence even to legitimize it in terms of some universal value. On the one hand this is an insistence upon (sometimes) primordial exceptionalism and uniqueness, and on the other it is an insistence upon either the European or the universal relevance of that exceptionalism. Since all these national myths are to a large extent dependent upon the exclusion of aspects of the historical legacy which do not correspond to the major objectives of the nation as these have been constructed by the national myth makers, they are extremely fragile and require the almost unconditional support of historians and the professionals in the humanities and social sciences which are the most important in myth making (sometimes linguists, sometimes ethnologists, sometimes both). Even if there is room for intellectual disputes within particular national cultures in the area, generally speaking there is almost no room for the systematic application of comparative approaches and methods across national borders in the immediate neighbourhood. Comparative approaches and methods seem to 'deconstruct' mythical and ideological appropriations of history, culture, language, and so on (there was not a single attempt to write a comparative history of the nations of Yugoslavia from 1945 to 1991).

Giving all that has happened in family memories in the past century in the areas that I am personally identified with, it seems to me that for many individuals, almost irrespective of education, maturity, and so on, it is almost impossible to cope with one's own experience in rational terms, much less to call into question the major trends of a particular national history. There have been too many tragedies, too many demonizations and exclusions. Living from day to day with all these memories, constantly under the pressure of different official and unofficial, public and private appropriations, is not easy. What does it mean to focus upon the past without having many opportunities for the future? Is this not the key question in all these discussions about the political uses of the past?

NOTE

1. Fernand Braudel, *The Mediterranean and the Mediterranean World in the Age of Philip II*, 2 Vols., trans. Sian Reynolds (New York, 1972–73).

Notes on Two Discordant Histories: Armenia during World War I

LUCETTE VALENSI

The historiography inspired by the Armenian question constitutes an extreme case of the political use of the past. While it would appear a simple matter to establish the 'historical facts' in connection with the fate of the Armenians of Anatolia during World War I, a specific series of events gave rise to two largely incompatible historiographic discourses.

The present situation has three characteristics. This was a historical moment that continues to affect the identity of both the Armenian and Turkish protagonists and their descendants and, more broadly, of the two national communities to which they belong. Furthermore, what is at stake in the conflict is ethical and political, and not merely historiographical. These two attributes characterize the history of numerous conflicts and civil wars that have put their stamp on the twentieth century. In the case of the Armenians, however, it is a third attribute that stands out. Generally, students of the history of violence in our recent history end up on some common ground, even while polemically confronting their sources or their narratives and even when they are historically and subjectively located in one of the camps engaged in the conflict. To cite just a few examples: Recent studies show that the historians of Palestine and of Israel, specialists in French colonial history and the National Liberation Movement in Algeria, analysts of World War II and the extermination of the Jews are by now able to construct, if not a homogeneous narrative, at least accounts which are compatible. They are able to confront each other – in other words, to talk to each other face to face. This does not hold for specialists on the Ottoman empire or modern Turkey and on the history of the Armenians. Where Armenia is involved, historians turn their backs on each other, playing from two discordant scores. While it is the political and national use of history that is at the centre of the historiographic conflict, it is precisely the resolution of this historiographic conflict that will lead to the suspension of hostilities.

We must, however, guard against the common notion that 'there are two sides to every story', including this history. Such a statement can only prolong a back-to-back stance and the continued generation of incompatible narratives. More important, the metaphor of 'two sides' refers to a political and economic act, the minting of coinage, and it would be preferable for the historiographic endeavour not to be inspired by such a metaphor. Historical truth is not for sale. It may well be a medium of exchange, intended for circulation, but it does not lend itself to manipulation, counterfeiting, or fluctuations in exchange rates. Besides, if the idea of 'sides' must be retained, then it would be best to posit more than two rather than the 'heads' or 'tails' of a coin. Similarly, we must beware of conceding that the golden mean has special virtues, with truth being held to lie between two positions both described as extremes.

Before specifying the issues at stake for the supporters of the various positions, the current historiographic configuration is briefly described. The survey covers three groups of studies: (1) histories produced by Armenian and pro-Armenian writers, (2) works which claim to be general histories of modern Turkey, produced by writers who are neither Turkish nor Armenian, and (3) histories written by Turks and pro-Turkish apologists. It should be borne in mind that the production of documents and the analysis of events started as early as 1915, and continued at a high level of intensity for the next decade and that the historiography and controversy have experienced a resurgence since 1965, the year marking the 50th anniversary of the genocide of the Armenians. Consequently, the foray into this vast bibliographical maze was not designed to rewrite this history in order to come up with an account which would be acceptable to all. Rather, the intention was, first, to try to gain a clearer view of the issue at stake[1] and then, if possible, to lay the groundwork (intellectual, if not yet sociopolitical) for a Turkish–Armenian debate and hence a confrontation between the two parties that might lead to a truce in the hostilities.

At the conclusion of this survey, we can try to answer to the following simple question: is there any minimal statement which could figure in both narratives? After attempting a number of formulations, the only possible version reads as follows: *Having decided on the deportation of the civilian Armenian population, the central government of the Ottoman empire implemented this policy between April and August 1915. The forced displacement, accompanied by massacres, led to the death of a large number of Armenians and the end of the Armenian presence in Anatolia.* I am, however, convinced that were I to submit this text to a mixed group of specialists in the field, they would reject it, being eager to specify the when and wherefore, the how and the details of the facts presented in this fashion. This would inevitably lead us to two entirely divergent accounts, summarized in utterances which would not be synonymous.

WHAT DO THE ARMENIAN HISTORIANS SAY?

Reduced to its bare bones, the Armenian narrative can be summarized as follows: when World War I broke out, the Ottoman empire threw in its lot with Germany, while the Armenian population remained massively loyalist and neutral (see the decision to this effect taken by the Congress of the Dashnaks in July 1914). The sporadic acts of resistance and guerrilla warfare were acts of self-defence triggered by the various repressive measures that were inflicted on the Armenians.

Beginning in April 1915, the Committee of Union and Progress (CUP), which had seized power following a coup d'état, implemented a policy of systematic extermination of the Armenian population – not only in North-Eastern Anatolia, near the Russian front and not only against Armenian activists but against the entire population. The war provided both a pretext and an opportunity to get rid of the Armenians, thereby definitively resolving the political question of their rights without the interference of the European powers.

Armenian historiography identifies the authors of this plan, in particular the triumvirate of Talaat (Minister of the Interior), Enver (Minister of War), and Djemal (Minister of the Navy), who worked through a special paramilitary organization. It details the geographic extent of the operation and its *modus operandi* (in each locality, the men were rounded up and executed; the rest of the population was rounded up and deported, accompanied by violence and under conditions such that the deportees were taken away to certain death). It spells out the chronology: it was a two-stage process, one in May–June 1915, for historic Armenia, and the second in the winter of 1915–16, for the Armenians of Cilicia and Western Anatolia. Only the Armenians of Istanbul, Smyrna, and Aleppo were spared, because of the presence in those cities of the Great Powers' consuls and other outside observers. Armenian historians estimate the number of victims at 1.5 million, or two-thirds of the Armenian population of the empire.

Recent studies focus on the factors underlying the discord between the Muslim majority population and the Armenians. These include such issues as the increasing social mobility of the latter, the rise of a national movement among the Armenians, and the call for (and recruitment of) Armenian volunteers by Russia after the beginning of the hostilities. These studies also highlight the contextual elements that heightened the distrust and then the hostility of the Turkish authorities, and in particular the territorial losses suffered by the Ottoman empire since the beginning of the nineteenth century, especially in its European provinces.

For all the sequences of this chronicle and for all the regions concerned, Armenian historians have collected and published as many documents and accounts as possible. There is nevertheless a tendency in the body of Armenian work to minimize Armenian separatist nationalist ambitions and the alliances struck to accomplish this end, as well as to belittle what the Turkish nationalists perceived (which in no way justifies the extermination of the civilian population). This tendency does not hold true for all historians. The work of Claire Mouradian in France and Richard Hovannisian in the United States for example, gives a fair account of the domestic and international dimensions of the question, locating the genocide in a broader setting and against a longer timeline.[2]

WHAT DOES TURKISH NATIONALIST HISTORIOGRAPHY SAY?

As in the Armenian case, an attempt to subsume all the Turkish nationalist works studied under a single category involves a certain degree of arbitrariness, since it neglects the specificities and focuses instead on points of convergence. The fact is that these convergent points do exist and that Turkish historiography on the period tends to combine – with variations – recurrent themes. Generally speaking, it establishes the guilt of the Armenians so as to justify the order of deportation and resettlement.

The major themes are:

1. Collusion with foreign powers bent on dismembering the Ottoman empire. Since the middle of the nineteenth century, Russia had been encouraging Armenian separatism. The Armenians, with the support of the Western powers, had already obtained a special status in the six provinces of North-Eastern Anatolia on the eve of the war.
2. Separatist Armenian nationalism for which the war was an opportunity to gain land. One variant of this theme is intercommunal tensions that since the end of the nineteenth century had brought local Muslims (particularly Kurds) into conflict with Christians, each side using violence. Another variant is the development of two rival nationalisms, one Turkish and Muslim, the other Armenian and Christian.
3. Treason from the very beginning of the war, the Armenians siding with Russia – going over to the Russian army across the border and initiating guerrilla warfare within the country.
4. Massacres and acts of violence carried out by the Armenians against the Muslim population.
5. Fabrication of documents after the war to justify the obtaining of political rights with the support of the Allies.

Turkish historiography exonerates the Ottoman and Turkish authorities: the decision to displace the population from the war zone to regions where they would no longer endanger Turkish defences was a measure of self-defence. It was temporary, and the Armenians were due to return home after the war. It was prepared in minute detail and organized so as to protect property and persons alike. No documents whatsoever have ever been found which prove that the decision to exterminate the Armenians was taken by the central government, the CUP, or any section whatsoever of its members.

What is denied in this historiography is:

1. The previous existence of Armenia as an identifiable historical territory and, as a corollary, the continuity of any specifically Armenian history.
2. The existence of the Armenians: They were a minority even in the six provinces, having already migrated before the war to the cities or to the West. Their numbers were far lower than all the estimates put forward.
3. The genocide: only certain regions were evacuated, with the intention of resettling the Armenian population. However high the death rate, it was a result of wartime: famine, illness, losses relating to general difficulties.
4. The extent of the losses compared with those of the Muslim Turks. The evaluation of the number of victims falls to 600,000, or even 200,000, compared with 2.5 million dead among the Muslim Turks of Anatolia, including 1,000,000 in the six provinces of the northeast.
5. The causes of these losses of life: in addition to the effects of the war, these losses were caused by the treachery of the Armenians who went over to the enemy camp.
6. The authenticity of the sources: they are biased, either as a result of the wartime situation, and hence suspect when they originate with the anti-Turkish Allied powers, or as a result of religious sympathies that benefit Christian rather than Muslim victims (at which point charges are levelled against the large numbers of sources originating with Christian missionaries in the field) or as a result of the political goals of the parties concerned – the Armenians and the countries trying to dismember the empire. German sources that confirm the extermination of the Armenians are therefore not taken into account, nor are the many specific accounts given by survivors.
7. The integrity of the courts martial held after the war and of the evidence mustered by the prosecution during these trials.

If we wished to draw up a list of the blind spots in Turkish publications, we would find they are riddled with them. This is a case of revisionism if not an open indictment of the victims. It is appropriate to use the concept of revisionism here – and it has already been used – because of the similarity of the procedures used in the Turkish arguments to those denying the extermination of the Jews and the existence of the gas chambers during

World War II. What makes this argumentation invalid is that it constitutes – as Copeaux has proven by a meticulous reading of Turkish output – a 'discourse of refutation' that insists on responding to the Armenian political and historiographic arguments at every turn. More important, every sequence in the denial is in part contradicted by the next sequence,[3] following the model of the famous story of the cooking pot, as reported by Freud.[4] The Turkish position has tended to become increasingly hardline in the past few decades. Official discourse and professional historiography continue to present a united front without any sign of dissociation. To the extent that any cracks are appearing on the nationalist front, they can be observed among certain journalists and in the world of publishing and in private conversations with Turkish historians and intellectuals, some of them possibly putting their lives on the line as a result of their statements or initiatives.[5]

WHAT DO OUTSIDE HISTORIANS SAY?

Among recent examples of the work of outside historians on the period, one position involves accusing the Armenians. The writings of Lowry, McCarthy, and Shaw and Shaw[6] have a distinctly polemical tone. In the name of a positivist approach, they denounce partisan history and take a strong stand in support of the Turkish nationalist version in even more forceful terms than the Turks themselves.

A second position is that of historians who indulge in euphemisms or evade the question. One example is Robert Mantran, who deals with this period but says nothing whatsoever about the Armenians. Another is Feroz Ahmad, who, while examining the social changes that took place during that period, addresses them in terms of social classes.[7] The existence of minorities and the problem of the relationships between them and between minorities and the majority population are therefore irrelevant. The Armenian question is scarcely mentioned, only passing reference being made to 'the deportation and the massacres of the Armenians'.

In the name of ostensible fairness, Benjamin Braude and Bernard Lewis[8] tend to put Armenians and Turks on an equal footing. Under the heading of intercommunal tensions, they equate the forces of the majority population, with the apparatus of a state buttressed by a fully equipped professional army, with the members of a minority of unarmed civilians. In their account, the Armenians 'perished': 'With the outbreak of WWI a terrible struggle between Turks and Armenians began. It ended with a disaster. In 1915, according to some observers, between one million and one and a half million Armenians perished. Once again the tragic themes of Armenian history were repeated'. In the case of Lewis, however, we can observe variations over time. In the first edition of his *Emergence of Modern Turkey,* referring to two irreconcilable nationalisms, he concluded that there had been a 'terrible holocaust' in which one and a half million Armenians died.[9] After revising this figure downward, he has subsequently dropped the notion of genocide, returning to the central argument of two nationalisms, one of which prevailed over the other.

The themes of 'intercommunal confrontation' and the cruelty of all wars are central in Paul Dumont and François Georgeon's reading of the events, which they summarize in a statement about 'the destruction of the Armenian communities of Eastern Anatolia'. However, this statement is somewhat diluted by the following assertion (based on military and demographic facts): 'However, it should be stressed that the Armenian communities are not the only ones which were wiped out by the scourge of war.'[10] While they admit that intentionality lay behind the deportation of the Armenians from the northeastern provinces in the spring of 1915, they nevertheless ascribe the high death toll not to any deliberate political act but to transport conditions and the circumstances inherent in any wartime situation.

The historian Erik Zürcher is in an isolated position in the midst of these outside historians. While drawing attention to the long-running and profound nature of the conflict of interests between Turks and Armenians, he firmly concludes that there was a deliberate policy of extermination orchestrated at the very heart of the Turkish political apparatus.[11]

Returning to the question of the political uses of the past, it will by now be obvious that historiographic work in this field is entirely on one side or the other of a political conflict that, while almost a century old, is still unresolved today. Beyond historical statements, what are the goals or expectations of those on both sides?

As in any historiographic work, Armenian scholars are pursuing cognitive objectives. For them, the issue is knowing the past in order to try to understand it and make it understood. In addition, through an analysis of the events that took place, they are seeking to exorcize the trauma experienced by the generation of their parents or grandparents and to enable the memory of this trauma to be passed on. Thus cognitive goals and the need for collective memory are closely linked.

The fact remains that the production of this knowledge cannot be separated from political expectations: political not in the sense of aiming at creating an Armenian political entity but insofar as they involve both the identity of the Armenians as a minority population and their coexistence with their neighbours. The process taking place in the Armenian diaspora is somewhat reminiscent of the experience of Diaspora Jews after the

Holocaust. The genocide of the Armenians has become both the founding element and the cement of contemporary Armenian identity, threatened as it is by geographical dispersion, the decline of the Armenian language, the weakening of religious affiliation, and successful integration into host societies. As with the Jews, the emergence (or reconstitution) of an educated élite also makes it possible for both a scholarly history (which is known to be the religion of the non-believer) and a fictional literature to flourish. Both these tendencies can be expected to develop as ways of maintaining Armenian identity in a diaspora situation.

Except for a minority activist group which has not yet declared this point of its programme null and void, the Armenians are no longer expecting territorial concessions.[12] Many acknowledge their dispersion and the irreversibility of the disappearance of any Armenian presence in Anatolia, and those who speak on their behalf have dropped any territorial claims in that region. A recent development actually favours this reorientation. The re-establishment of independence of the Republic of Armenia since the fall of the Soviet empire has allowed a different territorial reference and hence a new territorialization of identity. In this respect, developments among Armenians are somewhat reminiscent of what is happening to the Palestinians, whose historical existence in an ancestral land has long been denied but who, through the establishment of the Palestinian authority in an officially recognized area (while awaiting the creation of a Palestinian state), have acquired the possibility of a territorial foothold or anchor.

Generally, the Armenians no longer expect any financial compensation. Since international law has defined the concepts of genocide and crimes against humanity and international bodies have issued legal texts about acts of genocide with the goal of preventing and suppressing them, it is in this area that they have made their most sustained efforts. Historiographic activity is largely targeted at international bodies such as the United Nations and the European Parliament. The Armenians demand that the extermination of their people be defined as a genocide, the first such act of the twentieth century.[13] They are seeking Turkey's official recognition of this genocide and an expression of regret for it. They also expect a Turkish commitment to allow the expression of an Armenian culture in Turkey.

Armenians' generally successful integration into their host societies has given rise to a new demand directed not only at the descendants of yesterday's executioners but at the societies in which they are now living. What they are asking for is the public recognition and official commemoration of the genocide through its incorporation into the civic calendar. At the same time, this civic and ethical demand backs up the claims referred to above that are directed at modern Turkey.

At the moment, Turkish historians tend to share the dominant view in their country that supporting the national republican myth is one of the conditions for the existence of the republic founded by Atatürk. Abandoning this myth is tantamount to endangering national unity. In the same vein, recognizing Kurdish claims would jeopardize territorial unity and recognizing Islamist movements would undermine the secular foundations of the republic. Turkish historians who are specialists in the period remain attached to the overarching nationalist narrative constructed by Kemalism and instilled from earliest childhood onward, and in this setting they allocate no space to members of minorities.

The case of historians from the outside who more or less completely embrace the Turkish nationalist thesis is harder to understand, and certainly distinctions must be drawn among them. Are political factors also at work here, in particular since the postwar period, because of Turkey's strategic position in the context of the cold war on the one hand (being a Western bastion against the USSR), and the Middle East conflict, on the other (it is Israel's only ally in the region, against the bloc of Arab countries)? Do some historians, as specialists in modern Turkey, feel required to act as its spokespersons abroad, and do they consider empathy with the subject of their studies a condition for the latter? Has the dominant discourse, grounded in a state and its institutions (university and other), imposed itself on them, making them indifferent to or openly skeptical of the massive evidence connecting the massacres and the deportation of the Armenians? It should be remembered that since the resurgence of Armenian protests begun only in 1965, Turkish national historiography has had time to assert itself and overshadow the history of the vanquished. Be that as it may, the non-Turkish historians of contemporary Turkey are not alone in falling in line with the official version of history and identification with the subject they study.

In Turkey itself, the dissonant voices making themselves heard are responding, as in the first two cases, to issues of identity and to ethical and political concerns. They are, first, reclaiming the Armenians as part of their Turkish national heritage, thereby challenging the amputation performed by official discourse on the Ottoman and Turkish past. In this respect, the Armenians rejoin the company of other non-Muslim minorities who have disappeared from Turkish society and from its cultural heritage.

These voices are expressing the moral need to acknowledge the wrongs inflicted on the Armenians as a condition for reconciliation with themselves as well as with the Armenians. They are also asserting a fairly high degree of confidence in Turkish national unity by assuming that the latter can safely absorb a pluralism of opinions and beliefs, as well as a history which will no longer be a state catechism.

Thus in this case historiographic work is part and parcel of current political events and requires political initiatives. This does not mean that such initiatives are directly or exclusively the responsibility of the political authorities. They can also develop in the public space. One of the new features of our time is that this space has become transnational, profoundly modifying the relationships between actors and the resources that they can mobilize.[14] In any case, it is clear that, in this conflict and the quest for a solution to it, historians, who are entitled to have their say, using the tools of their trade, are also required to intervene in their capacity as citizens.

Translated by Ruth Morris

NOTES

1. Analyses of this type have already been attempted; see in particular Gwynne Dyer, 'Turkish "Falsifiers" and Armenian "Deceivers": Historiography and the Armenian Massacres", *Middle Eastern Studies*, 1 (12 Jan. 1976), pp.99–107; Etienne Copeaux, *Espaces et temps de la nation turque: Analyse d'une historiographie nationaliste, 1931–1993* (Paris, 1997).
2. Claire Mouradian, *L'Arménie* (Paris, 1995); Richard G. Hovannisian (ed.), *The Armenian Genocide: History, Politics, Ethics* (New York, 1992); idem., *The Armenian Genocide in Perspective* (New Brunswick, NJ, and Oxford, 1986); idem., *The Armenian People from Ancient to Modern Times*, Vol. 2 (New York, 1997).
3. Such forms of denial can also be found in other political-historiographic debates, particularly on the existence of Palestine (as a historical territory, as a people and nation, etc.).
4. See Nadine Fresco, 'Les redressers de morts', *Les Temps modernes* (June 1980), pp.2150–211, to my knowledge the first scholarly reference to S. Freud, *Le mot d'ésprit et ses rapports avec l'inconscient* (Paris, 1969), pp.89–90. Freud reports the story, which he calls a sophism 'about which we laughed heartily, although one questions its character as a witticism: A borrowed from B a copper cooking pot; when he gave it back, B complained that the cooking pot had a big hole in it, which meant it could no longer be used. This was A's reply: "First, I never borrowed the cooking pot from B; secondly, the pot had a hole when I borrowed it; thirdly, I gave the pot back undamaged." Each of these objections is valid on its own, but when taken together each of them excludes the other.' On similar sophisms, see Pierre Vidal-Naquet, 'Un Eichman de papier', in *Les Juifs, la mémoire et le présent* (Paris, 1981), pp.193–272.
5. I will refer here simply to the work of Taner Akçam, *Türk Ulusal Kimligi ve Erment Sorunu* (Istanbul, 1992) and the Editions Belge International.
6. Justin McCarthy, *Muslims and Minorities: The Population of Ottoman Anatolia and the End of the Empire* (New York and London, 1983); Stanford J. Shaw and Ezel Kural Shaw, *History of the Ottoman Empire and Modern Turkey*, Vol. 2, *Reform, Revolution and Republic: The Rise of Modern Turkey, 1808–1975* (Cambridge, London and New York, 1976).
7. Robert Mantran, *Histoire de la Turquie* (Paris, 4th Edn. 1975); Feroz Ahmad, *The Making of Modern Turkey* (London and New York, 1993).
8. Benjamin Braude and Bernard Lewis (eds.), *Christians and Jews in the Ottoman Empire*, Vol. 1 (New York and London, 1982).

9. Bernard Lewis, *The Emergence of Modern Turkey* (London and New York, 1961).
10. Paul Dumont and François Georgeon, 'La mort d'un empire (1908–1923)', in Robert Mantran (ed.), *Histoire de l'Empire ottoman* (Paris, 1989), pp.577–648.
11. Erik J. Zürcher, *Turkey: A Modern History* (London and New York, 2nd Edn. 1997).
12. Just as the practice of terrorism has not been declared null and void even though it has come to an end after targeting Turkish diplomats abroad and other symbolic representatives of official Turkey since the 1970s.
13. It obviously goes without saying that such a step would go far beyond the Armenian case, creating a basic precedent: if the goals of international law on genocide are indeed repression and prevention, the denial of the first act of genocide of our century would preclude their achievement.
14. I would like to thank Nilüfer Gölé for drawing my attention to this aspect.

SELECTED BIBLIOGRAPHY

This paper is a discussion of the present historiography on the period of the Armenian genocide. To facilitate access to this discussion a bibliographical list is hereby appended.

Armenians in the Ottoman Empire and Modern Turkey, 112–1926 (Istanbul, 1984).

Documents on Ottoman-Armenians, 2 vols. (n.d., published by Turkey's Prime Minister's Office).

The Turco-Armenian Question: The Turkish Point of View (Constantinople, 1919).

Tribunal permanent des peuples. Le crime de silence: Le génocide des Arméniens, preface by P. Vidal-Naquet (Paris, 1984).

Feroz Ahmad, *The Making of Modern Turkey* (London and New York, 1993).

Taner Akcam, *Türk Ulusal Kimligi ve Erment Sorunu* (Istanbul, 1992) (Critical review by Mihran Dabag, 'Le traumatisme des bourreaux: à propos du livre de Taner Akçam', in *Revue du Monde arménien modern et contemporain*, 1 (1994), pp.10–108. Another critical review by Hilar Kaiser, in *Journal of the Society for Armenian Studies*, 8 (1995), pp.205–9).

Varoujan Attarian, *Le génocide des Arméniens devant l'ONU* (Brussels, 1977).

Alessio Bombaci and Standford J. Shaw, *L'Impero ottomano* (Turin, 1981).

Benjamin Braude and Bernard Lewis (eds.), *Christians and Jews in the Ottoman Empire*, Vol. 1 (New York and London, 1982).

Etienne Copeaux, *Espaces et temps de la nation turque: Analyse d'une historiographie nationaliste, 1931–1993* (Paris, 1997).

Vhakn N. Dadrian, 'The Naim-Andonian Documents on the WWI Destruction of Ottoman Armenians: The Anatomy of a Gencoide', *IJMES*, 18 (1986), pp.311–60.

——— *Autopsie du génocide arménien* (Brussels, 1989).

Paul Dumont and François Georgeon, 'La mort d'un Empire (1908–1923)', in Robert Mantran (ed.), *Histoire de l'Empire ottoman* (Paris, 1989), pp.577–648.

Gwynne Dyer, 'Turkish "Falsifiers" and Armenian "Deceivers": Historiography and the Armenian Massacres', *Middle Eastern Studies*, 12/1 (Jan. 1976), pp.99–107.

Richard G. Hovannisian (ed.), *The Armenian Genocide. History, Politics, Ethics* (New York, 1992).

——— *The Armenian Genocide in Perspective* (New Brunswick and Oxford, 1986).

——— *The Armenian People from Ancient to Modern Times*, Vol. 2 (New York, 1997).

Johannes Lepsius, *Archives du génocide des Arméniens. Recueil de documents diplomatiques allemands extraits de Deutschland und Armenien (1914–1918)* (Paris, 1986).

Bernard Lewis, *The Emergence of Modern Turkey* (1961).
Robert Mantran, *Histoire de la Turquie* (Paris, 4th Edn. 1975).
Justin McCarthy, *Muslims and Minorities: The Population of Ottoman Anatolia and the End of the Empire* (New York and London, 1983).
Claire Mouradian, *L'Arménie* (Paris, 1995).
Mim Kemâl Öke, *The Armenian Question. 1914–1923* (Oxford, 1988).
Stanford J. Shaw and Ezel Kural Shaw, *History of the Ottoman Empire and Modern Turkey. Vol. II, Reform, Revolution and Republic: The Rise of Modern Turkey, 1808–1975* (Cambridge, London and New York, 1976).
Anahide Ter Minassian, 'Mouch 1915 selon Alma Johannson', *Haigazian Armenological Review*, 15 (1995), pp.57–85.
Erik J. Zürcher, *Turkey, A Modern History* (London and New York, 2nd Edn. 1997).

The Distant Past: On the Political Use of History

GIOVANNI LEVI

Noting the loss of the meaning of history through which Marxism-Leninism and – more generally – democratic thought 'had claimed to provide democratic optimism with the guarantee of science', François Furet concluded *Le passé d'une illusion* by stating that 'the idea of another society has become practically impossible to imagine ... Here we are, condemned to live in the world in which we live!'[1] And then he added:

> If capitalism has become the future of socialism, if the middle-class world is to take over from that of the "proletarian revolution", what will happen to this assurance about time? The inversion of the canonical priorities is undoing the way ages interlock on the road of progress. History again becomes a tunnel that mankind enters in darkness, not knowing where its actions will take it, uncertain as to its destiny, deprived of the illusory security of a knowledge of what it is doing. Bereft of God, the democratic individual sees the divinity of history trembling on its foundations at this century's close ... In his mind, this threat of uncertainty goes hand in hand with the outrage of a foreclosed future.[2]

Despite everything, what prevails is an optimistic outlook: the end of an illusion compels us to come to terms with a more realistic and more human world, devoid of messianism. But Furet's analysis also touches – albeit *en passant* – on a substantial question: even history, a political weapon used to give meaning to the world of the past according to a logic of the present, has suddenly lost its certainties. It is this aspect of the question that needs to be examined with a less optimistic eye. It is not only for an understanding of the future that new instruments are required; while robust forms of power are consolidating their economic and ideological domination, the significance of the past must also be reestablished. The fact is that ideological disarmament is not a general phenomenon: only one of the parties has suffered a loss of meaning. In this unequal situation, a new political use of history is taking hold, an invasive form which finds historians particularly uncertain and defenceless.[3] The foundations and the scope of the profession have changed more than has been recognized.

It would be absurd to consider the political use of history something new. By definition, history's character as a civic science makes it a political activity. Whether it is scrutinizing individual or local phenomena, groups, institutions, or nations, or, ultimately, the formation of states and the development of cultures, it seems impossible to detach it from the civic aspect of defining identities, whether one's own or those of others. Thus history has always produced views of the world indissociably linked with a political element whose use, whether conscious or unconscious, was in any case inevitable. This use has a history of its own that is worth examining, a history made up of a number of elements foremost of which is the relationship between the historian and a public that changes over time.

History has faced this problem in implicit fashion, maintaining a tone which, to paraphrase James Clifford, we might call authoritarian.[4] It has constructed a peremptory rhetoric for presenting itself to its readers, a rhetoric implying the idea of an objective reconstruction of the facts in the broad sense, as if the object of history were to reconstruct the way that things occurred – as if a necessary relationship existed between text and reality in which the historical text represented a definite world endowed with meaning. This authoritarian image conceals one of the most widespread implicit aspects of the ability to persuade, the one most solidly rooted in historical shared meaning: readers ask the historian many things but assume that what they are told is true. It is this that makes it possible to tell deliberate untruths and be believed. In addition, the extraordinary transformation brought about by the fall of the Soviet system and the end of bipolarism has created the bewildered expectation of a rereading of history, a revision which calls for new interpretive tools but has not lost this idea of the historian's scientific authority.

Hence the new political use of history and its meaning is a matter not of the seriousness of the discussion but of the rhetoric employed in addressing a historical tradition. To demonstrate this, we take an example which is particularly distressing from the scientific point of view.

In his introduction to the memoirs of two Italians who took part in the Spanish Civil War – Giuliano Bonfante, who left the Republican front in 1937, and Edgar Sogno, a volunteer in Franco's forces from 1938 onwards – Sergio Romano, an Italian diplomat and journalist (generally presented as a historian), justifies Franco's uprising as a response to communism and Republican violence rather than considering it the cause of the Communists' gradual preeminence within the anti-Franco front: 'Thus the war stopped being a war between fascism and anti-fascism, becoming instead a war between fascism and communism.'[5] However, according to Romano Franco 'was not a fascist ... He was authoritarian, reactionary, a bigot, ruthless. But he was Spanish'.[6] Franco was perceptive in failing to respond to the Axis powers' requests to intervene, thereby keeping Spain out of World War II. He was

> cruel, vain, irritable, but he never did to Spanish society what people like Gottwald, Novotny, Rakosi, Dimitrov, Grotowohl, Gheorghiu-Dej, Ceaucescu, and the other postwar communist leaders did to their own countries' societies. Confirmation of this is provided by the fact that, in the last phase of Franco's life and immediately after his death, it was very clear that, despite the dictatorship, Spain had preserved the vigour and power it needed for its political and economic future. Hence, in the long run and with hindsight, one is tempted to conclude that Bonfante was right to abandon the Party in 1937 and that Sogno was not wrong to enter the arena in 1938.[7]

There is nothing brilliant here – only simplifications, falsifications, propaganda. Yet this was a matter of great importance, and triggered an enormous debate in public opinion and the press but also among professional historians.[8] At the same time, it was a debate which, ultimately, lacked teeth. Some participants tried to clarify things, describing how matters had developed – explaining that in 1936 the Communists had been a tiny minority in the Spanish parliament and thus refuting the obvious absurdity of justifying Francoism as a response to communism, along the lines of Nolte's theses. Others expressed indignation at the manipulation of the facts, the extraordinary simplification, the ignorance of the ferocity of Francoism both during and after the Civil War. But the machinery of persuasion had been set in motion, and neither explanations nor clarifications would do any good: in this case as in others, the complexity of the historical facts and their real meaning were manipulated in such a way that people could state indifferently that it was impossible to come down clearly on one side or the other. Good is to be found in everything, but, more generally, the whole of history is the bearer of evil. As can be seen, all of the main elements of the dominant historical tradition were present: no position was clearly positive (Franco was cruel, the Republicans were bloodthirsty and dominated by communism – and what was worse than communism in the twentieth century?); both parties came together under the same pallid gaze, made up of scepticism and uncertainty, which paralyzed all choices and all stances (the only meaningful tool for appraisal being knowledge with hindsight).

It is no coincidence that the volume appeared as a supplement to *Liberal*, a weekly financed by Cesare Romiti, former chairman of Fiat and an interesting *esirg ecnenim* in political and economic life, both Italian and Spanish. In June 1998, when Romano published his little volume, Romiti completed his 25 years as chairman of Fiat and became chairman of RCS-

Rizzoli, which among other ventures owned two major daily newspapers, the *Corriere della Sera* and *El Mundo*. RCS-Rizzoli was one of the standard bearers of the Italian–Spanish cooperation, presented as a counterweight to Franco-German domination of Europe at the same time that Iveco was planning a large scale truck factory in Catalonia, Italian and Spanish banks were merging, and the Italian book industry was making inroads into the Spanish market. These Italian conservatives (in addition to Romiti,[9] even Berlusconi and Casini made comments along similar lines) are constantly presenting Aznar's Spain as an example for both Italy and Europe. Concealed beneath improbable and superficial historical interpretations is a propaganda campaign designed to suggest a continuity between Francoism and current developments, ignoring the intervening 20 years of Socialist government, its dangerous state socialism, and its social-welfare policy. This is an attempt to exorcise the image of a dynamic Spain which is nevertheless threatened by a past with which accounts have not been settled. Italian Fascism, along with Francoism, has managed to become more democratic and modern: in hindsight, both were minor evils directed against the communist peril and opened the way for economic development and neoliberalism. *Post hoc ergo propter hoc.*

This is an extreme example, showing the journalistic use of the past and therefore lacking direct ties with scientific debate and research. Yet it is a debate with great resonance which clearly illustrates the means and aims of the political use of the past and, at the same time, the difficulty of protecting oneself against practices of this nature using standard research tools. On this basis, we now address a specific question: Are there significant innovations in the political use of history today?

To start with, there is one striking innovation: the relationship between history and its readers has changed because book-based communication has lost the quasi-monopoly which it had gradually gained with the spread of the printed word. True, in the past, other forms of transmitting historical knowledge also played a role: pictures, for example, or oral transmission. But there is no denying the fact that for a long time printing, widespread literacy, mass education, and the declining cost of books all played a key role in giving historical production fundamental political weight in the construction of identity-based ideologies, in the states of the modern and contemporary period. Today other sources of information compete with books and are gradually forcing historical research to modify the way in which it confronts a historical tradition which has itself changed radically.

My impression is that professional historians have not fully recognized this, and therefore have not addressed it to any great extent. Often, it is true, complaints are heard about the decline in readership, and the production of history books requires ever larger subsidies because their sales are not sufficient to provide economic justification for their publication. But it seems there is no appreciation of the radical changes that have taken place in the very system of communicating research results. Putting it bluntly, newspapers, television, and other means of communication today provide information whose inherent qualities – simplification and speed – differ very markedly from those of history but nevertheless have an impact on the same group of consumers, thereby modifying the market.

School has been *the* place for popularizing knowledge of history, *the* place for the civic and political use of history, *the* place the socialization of young people through the transmission of identity models shaped by the historical events which have formed nations. But, just as the mode of socialization has changed, with a reduction in the role of the family and an increase in the role of the peer group, so too, side by side with the school, the cinema, television, the Internet, and newspapers have created a new and powerful array of models. This array has transformed the very role of the school, which is now required to come to grips with a of information which is both exponentially larger and uncontrolled.

It is not at all surprising that, in recent years, public debate about the socializing uses of history in France, Italy, and Spain, has led to a profound transformation of school curricula. In all three countries the upshot has been paradoxical: history has not been viewed as a tool for an in-depth, long term understanding of the process by which national realities and complex changes in the world have come about. As a result, it has not been given a problem-oriented reading that takes account of chronologies and complex developments. Rather, borne along by a historical tradition marked by an emphasis on the factual and the short-term, it has been transformed by a fact-oriented approach – the idea being that recent facts are by definition, more important than those of the past, 'given the pedagogical and cultural requirement to spend more time dealing with recent events …, which should benefit from a greater abundance of particulars and references'.[10] This has led to an expansion of the contemporary and an over-simplification of the more remote past: history has been turned into news.

This perspective does not just propose an infinite and impossible quest for the facts. The overarching idea it reflects is that of an ever more uniform world, in which different countries' anthropological and cultural characteristics must be minimized – a world which facilitates the transcending of differences and instances of backwardness in respect of a single model of a European citizen. But this overlooks the fact that the problem is deep-seated differences, rather than superficial congruities and immediate correspondences and that only with an understanding of the real dimensions and scale of social and cultural realities is it possible to coordinate different values – something that simplification and levelling do not allow for. In my opinion, all one has to do is to reflect on the recent events in the Balkans or the difficulties with the European monetary unit to realize that ethnic, religious, and national differences react wildly to the imposition of uniform models, which, riding roughshod over distinctive features, help to strengthen these very differences.

It is not only information methods which are affected by these changes: memory, too, has changed. Memory has all too often been simplistically contrasted with oblivion, as if the war of representations of the past could be reduced to the conflict between what one chooses to remember and what one wishes to erase. It is no coincidence that much of the revisionist debate has seemingly centred around the need for a balanced solution to exorcize those unacceptable pasts making Germany guilty because of Nazism, imposing silence about the Vichy period, considering Fascism a bizarre digression in the history and conscience of the majority of the Italian people, and covering the Spanish Civil War and Francoism with a resounding silence. Silence was not enough: what was required was normalization, abandoning the Manichean distinction between the positive conquerors and the negative vanquished. Revisionism did not draw its strength from contemporary facts alone: other past facts were presented ambiguously to memory and rearranged so as to favour oblivion. Here a good example is the apology which the pope has proposed to offer for the Inquisition. The final treatment of this matter has been postponed until the jubilee year, and to date it has produced only factual justifications relating to the inquisitors' compliance with the rules, their clemency, and the fact that they acted with great propriety compared with the temporal courts.

However, this is not just a question of memory or oblivion but a question of a change in memory itself, which has become something other than what it was, both collective and social – attributes which are normally thought of in connection with history. Memory has expanded to the extent that it has produced what Bion has called an 'obstruction', making it impossible to intuit unknown phenomena: an overabundance of memory is also an overabundance of conformism, a saturation which impedes judgement and criticism.[11] And, at the same time, the triumphal process of the individualizing and privatizing of experience has produced a fragmented, individualized memory. This is each individual's memory, not that of a group or a people: no longer a communicable history but an autobiography, no longer society's past but a myriad of separate fragments and objects, 'things which are represented by the everyday imagination, sustained by books, films, and vague myths. It slips, inevitably, towards simplification and stereotyping', the result of the separation and drift which memory inevitably brings about between the experiences of different individuals and different generations.[12]

Underlying this is a powerful, conscious ideology which exalts only the positive aspects of asserting the individual's autonomy in the modern state. To illustrate this we offer a second example of the political use of history. In this instance, it is not revisionism but a more complex and more subtle operation of ideologically oriented history. That is, the monumental research project – more than ten volumes – which the European Science Foundation has promoted and financed on the origins of the modern state in Europe from the thirteenth to the eighteenth century.[13] Based on an explicit desire to make political use of history, it was intended to show the inescapability of a specific form of a modern state, relative to which deviations and delays were pathologies and alternatives only instances of pointless resistance. One of the volumes is entitled 'The Individual in Theory and Practice'.[14] The thesis advanced in the introduction by the volume's editor, Janet Coleman, is as follows: that in European history an unconscious and hence non-teleological process has, irrespective of everything which has occurred, led to a uniform process of individualization. In this way a space has emerged which is specific to the individual, made up of important shared attributes which have generated a common 'European experience'.

> It is in this free and indeterminate space, protected by law from the interference of the State or any other individual, that the unique character of the individual best develops and flourishes in the modern liberal state ... Complete submission to the state's laws guarantees the modern citizen complete inner freedom as an individual once he governs himself and is autonomous.[15]

Despite the triteness of the thesis, what is striking – in this as in the entire area addressed by the collection – is the essentially apologetic tone and the inevitability aspect of the processes: history has abandoned the role of the science of specific differences in order to become the builder of improbable forms of approval. Thus, while all the ever stronger powers elude democratic control – while each of us sees that it is ever more difficult to oppose, by means of the fragile weapon of the vote, the economic and political decisions of a world which stresses interdependence and global characteristics – what is constantly being proposed to us is the end of ideologies and the triumph of the individual, the end of history under liberal capitalism and the affirmation of fragmented memory. Tocqueville put it trenchantly: 'Not only does democracy make each man forget his ancestors: it hides his descendants from him, and separates him from his contemporaries; it constantly brings him back to himself alone, threatening to ultimately confine him entirely in the solitude of his own heart'.[16]

It is therefore an individualized memory, replete with information but fragmented, which historians find among their readers: a memory with a tendency to simplify, to convert into stereotypes, the expression of a disjointed society which has weakened the complex meaning of any collective memory or, better, which is sensitive to simplified forms of representing the past made up of slogans and myths that are devoid of real content but no less powerful or galvanizing or, alternatively, less paralyzing.

It is precisely in this superposing of fragments and memory that we find some of the ambiguities characteristic of the use of oral sources: for many historians, the loss of collective sense or meaning of the past has made it possible to recover subjective views which generally express disintegration rather than a multiplicity of viewpoints. Of course this point is not made in order to reject wholesale the use of oral sources, but simply to emphasize that when they are used it must be recognized that they have no special privilege and do not provide us with immediate access to reality: rather, they tend to hide it from us because of their ability to generate miscommunication, influenced by emotionalism rather than a critical eye. Without a doubt, positive uses exist: many of the recent studies of Nazi massacres in Italy have helped to show us how individual memory, through a settling effect, the influence of the media, and stylization, has constructed distorted images of the past weighed down by an ideology which decontextualizes the past in order to manipulate it in a more or less conscious fashion.[17]

It may be needless to point out that the end of bipolarism in world politics has profoundly altered the topics and trends of historical research. Entire areas (such as the history of the labour movement) have gradually been wiped out or marginalized, and a general climate of uncertainty has swept over historians' labours. The end of the Soviet system and the image of the market economy as the only realistic perspective for any institutional organization, even going beyond the neoliberal extremists, have eliminated a goodly number of perspectives which made social and cultural conflict the focus of historians' attention. Social solidarity, which made the adoption of political positions seemingly automatic, has become far less of a foregone conclusion, and in recent discussions the very meaning of right and left – allusive but immediately perceptible – has become disordered. Out of the blue, there is an absence of references and obvious facts, of moral and cultural values, unless tendered by historians, at least in the shared meaning of the past. As at all moments of crisis and reordering, there is undoubtedly a positive aspect to this: the schemas and falsifications which have retained abusive power in the shared culture are vanishing. But the immediate damage caused is deep-seated and unmistakable: for the time being, it is encountering little opposition because it is difficult for a science weakened by a profound crisis to address it. If we consider the role played by historical facts in today's political debate, we are struck by the confusion and uncertainty that are fostered by this climate of doubt and weakness: localism and nationalism, acts of violence, and inequalities are invading the byways which have been left open because historiography cannot play its civic role.

The didactic way in which history is being used in many countries has often been based on the idea that nations are born out of violence, not only in their defence against outside enemies but also in civil war, which has allowed the victorious party's own principles to prevail. It is with this idea that young Americans have been raised concerning the American Revolution, British young people with regard to the English Civil War, or French young people with regard to the French Revolution. However, this model cannot be generalized. It is this problem which arises when it comes to acknowledging that the Italian Risorgimento was not only a war against Austria but also a war against the pope and that Italy's Resistance movement was a civil war waged by part of the population against another rather than by all Italians against a tiny minority of Fascists. The upshot has been serious damage to Italy's ability to construct strong founding myths. Fascism itself, in order not to offend the Catholics, has had to choose its own – highly unlikely – basic myths, going back to ancient Rome or, a pinch, to the Great War against Austria and not to the Risorgimento.

Today's instances of revisionism, in contrast, follow a contrasting procedure. Their goal is not to reassess movements, leading figures, or periods, but rather to strip the past of its value. The common theme has been to make the parties in conflict equal – and to make both of them negative. In a just but ambiguous war against Manichean readings of history, everything which had appeared to be innovative has been shown to have had its negative aspects. Nolte did not argue his theses on the basis of a reevaluation of Nazism; nor was it a reevaluation of Fascism which led to the demonstration of the acts of violence perpetrated by the Resistance in Italy. The resulting picture of the past is not an inverted interpretation but rather a levelling out of positions, all of which are viewed as negative. The past is laden with hideousness.

It is in this regard that the Catholic Church's current political use of history appears significant. Two examples are particularly indicative of an instrumentalization of the facts of the past; they are also indicative of the effects of the disinformation produced by the press and television in summarizing texts, turning them into brief news items which are repeated and committed to memory, far more than the content or the real meaning of the church's revision of the past.

The process of rewriting history and proposing models of saintliness represented by the innumerable decisions on beatification of recent years deserves a more detailed analysis than can be given here. However, it is obvious that an intensive production of symbols, laden with consequences, is taking place. For example, what was the message that the Vatican wished to convey by beatifying Cardinal Stepinač? Having been one of the proponents of the policy which contributed to the disintegration of Yugoslavia, with the early recognition of Croatian autonomy, on 8 March 1999 John Paul II beatified Cardinal Stepinač, the symbol of Croatian anti-Titoism but also ambiguously linked with the policies and crimes of Ante Pavelič. Stepinač has never condemned the Croatian Fascists' ferocious practices, and he has remained silent about the involvement of members of the Croatian Catholic clergy in the massacres of resistance fighters and Orthodox Christians perpetrated by the Ustashi and in the operation of concentration camps at Jasenovaæ and elsewhere.[18]

A second example involves a document, which is itself significant; it also involves the gap between the image widely held by public opinion and the content of the text. After a vigorous press campaign, which created high expectations concerning a revision of the Vatican's attitude during the Shoah (Holocaust), on 16 March 1998 the Vatican Committee for Religious Relations with the Jews published the document called *We Remember: A Reflection on the Shoah.*[19] In this extraordinary and ambiguous text, the extermination of the Jews is roundly and unhesitatingly condemned; at the same time, the moral responsibility of the church in not having resolutely opposed the crime is set within an array of ambiguities and justifications. A number of points seem particularly important. Starting from the distinction between anti-semitism and anti-Judaism, the document acknowledges that anti-Judaism has sometimes 'unfortunately' even involved Christians. But Nazi anti-semitism was a doctrine with neo-pagan roots because it 'refused to acknowledge all transcendent realities as the source of life and the criterion of moral good'. Its anti-semitism was 'rooted outside of Christianity, and, in pursuing its goals, it did not hesitate to oppose the Church and to persecute her members also'. A subtle appropriation of the martyrdom of others confirms the practice of introducing Catholic symbols at Auschwitz.

The document goes on to wonder 'whether the Nazi persecution of the Jews was not facilitated by the prejudices entrenched in a certain number of Christian minds and hearts'. There is, however, no answer to this question: 'Any answer to this question must take account of the fact that we are addressing the history of people's attitudes [the church as an institution was remote at that time] and their ways of thinking, which are subject to manifold influences'. And in addition, since many were unaware of the

Final Solution, others were frightened, and yet others benefited from the situation, 'an answer must be given to each individual case'.

Misdeeds were committed by Western countries with a Christian tradition and by individuals; but there is no reference to the attitude of the church as an institution, which does not reappear until mention is made of qualities 'including what Pope Pius XIII did personally or through his intermediaries in order to save hundreds of thousands of Jewish lives'. Then comes John Paul II's address to the Strasbourg Jewish community: 'I once again before you repeat our most earnest condemnation of anti-semitism and racism, which are utterly at variance with the principles of Christianity.' And nevertheless, the document goes on immediately to equate the Shoah with 'all forms of genocide, as well as the racist ideologies which cause them':

> We refer here in particular to the massacre of the Armenians, the countless victims in Ukraine in the 1930s, the genocide of the Gypsies, which was also the result of racist ideas, and similar tragedies which took place in America, Africa, and the Balkans. Nor do we forget the millions of victims of totalitarian ideology in the Soviet Union, China, Cambodia, and elsewhere. We also do not forget the tragedy of the Middle East.

And, to complete this reworking, in which meanings are intertwined and misdeeds are equated, the document concludes, almost incredibly: 'We hope to transform the awareness of past sins into a firm resolution to construct a new future in which there will no longer be any anti-Judaism among the Christians nor anti-Christian sentiments among the Jews.'

Over and above the suggestive comparisons (Jewish martyr–Christian martyr; Pius XII's role as a saviour, with no reference to criticism for his failure to take action; likening the genocides; comparing genocides and the Middle East question; Christian misdeeds–Jewish misdeeds), what we have here is an extreme rereading of the past. The resultant picture is of a past is rife with evil, but it is impossible to pinpoint any source of that evil other than the deniers of the transcendent origin of life and morality, hence the Nazis and the Communists. The others all had certain faults, but these were human ones: the Ustashi, who perpetrated massacres without denying God, if not in His name; the Jews for having anti-Christian sentiments; the Christians for an anti-Judaism which must nevertheless be put in context and understood in each individual instance. Men are known to be sinners.

This last pontificate has changed the political role of the church. It wishes to impart a new image in which the church would appear as a whole: the slightest hint of any political position has vanished. The church has given up its partisan behaviour (the all-Catholic party no longer exists) and now presents itself as above partiality or bias. But this historical vision also strips history of importance. The past is merely the place of sin and confusion, where everyone, and hence no one, is guilty – neither Stepinač nor Pius XII, both beatified for having testified as to the Catholic truth, always choosing the inevitable path of the lesser evil in a world of violence and sin.

Three very different examples of the political use of history have been chosen, without trying to present all types. It does not seem possible to identify a common core which has profoundly marked the reception of the results of historical research. The alleged end of ideologies is merely a suspension of historical reason, which, helpless, opens its door to the triumph of those selfsame ideologies: irrationalism, nationalism, neoliberalism, religious fundamentalism. History is being manipulated and used, while the voices of historians have become muffled and distant. Neither fragmented memory nor the school nor the communications media can apply their slow and uncertain procedures. This situation is in urgent need of discussion.

Translated by Ruth Morris

NOTES

1. F. Furet, *Le passé d'une illusion: Essai sur l'idée communiste au XXe siècle* (Paris, 1995), p.809.
2. Ibid., p.808.
3. An interesting example is the weakness and indecision with which Furet himself refutes two central points in Nolte's theses – the chronological priority and hence the causal role of Bolshevism relative to Nazism and the identification of a rational nucleus in Nazi anti-semitism – in their recently published correspondence: F. Furet and E. Nolte, *XX secolo: Per leggere il Novecento fuori dai luoghi comuni* (Rome, 1997).
4. J. Clifford, 'On Ethnographic Authority', *Representations*, 10/1 (1983), pp.118–46.
5. *Due fronti: La guerra di Spagna nei ricordi personali di opposti combattenti di sessant'anni* (Florence, 1998), p.xiii. A new version appeared a few weeks later, comprising part of the debate and a reply by Romano.
6. Ibid., p.197.
7. Ibid., p.xv.
8. Contributors to the debate include M. Pirani (*La Repubblica*, 13 and 21 May 1998), R. Foa (*L'Unità*, 15 May), B. Spinelli (*La Stampa*, 17 and 24 May), N. Aiello (interviewer: Valiani, *La Repubblica,* 20 May), E. Sogno (*La Stampa*, 21 May), G. Ranzato (*La Repubblica*, 25 May), S. Romano (*Corriere della Sera*, 6 June), E. Deaglio (*Diario*, 24–30 June), M.A. Maciocchi (*El Pais*, 26 June), S. Viola (*La Stampa*, 28 June), I. Montanelli (*Corriere della Sera*, 30 June), M. Veneziani (*Il Giornale*, 30 June), F. Perfetti (*Avvenire*, 30 June), A. Tabucchi (*Corriere della Sera*, 30 June and 27 July), P. L. Battista (*La Stampa*, 1 July), M. Brambilla (*Corriere della Sera*, 2 July), A Panebianco (*Corriere della Sera*, 4 July), P. Ostellino (*Corriere della Sera*, 5 July), G.P. Pasa (*L'Espresso*, 9 July), E. Bettiza (*La Stampa*,

11 July), F. Adornato (*Liberal*, 16 July), S. Julià (*Babelia*, 18 July), A. Botti (*El Pais*, 10 Aug.). Further names could undoubtedly be added to the list.

9. Cf., for example, the interview given to *La Stampa* (20 May, 1998), the statements on television and reproduced in the newspapers of 23 Sept. 1998, and the interview in *La Repubblica* (31 Dec. 1998).
10. This is the upshot of Decree No. 682, dated 4 Nov. 1996, of the Italian Ministry of Education, on 'modifications of the provisions concerning the annual subdivision of the history program', stipulating that, in all kinds of schools, the last year will be devoted solely to the twentieth century.
11. W.R. Bion, *Group and Organization Studies* (Colchester, 1974), pp.16–17.
12. P. Levi, *I sommersi e i ssalvati* (Turin, 1986), p.128.
13. Cf. the detailed presentation given by J.-P. Genet, 'La genèse de l'Etat moderne: Les enjeux d'un programme de recherche', *Actes de la Recherche en Sciences Sociales* (Paris), No.118 (1997), pp.3–18. I have myself discussed this project in 'The Origins of the Modern State and the Microhistorical Perspective', in J. Schlumbohm (ed.), *Mikrogeschichte/ Makrogeschichte: Komplementar oder incommensurabel?* (Göttingen, 1998), pp.53–82.
14. J. Coleman (ed.), *L'individu dans la théorie et dans la pratique* (Paris, 1996).
15. Ibid., p.xviii.
16. A. de Tocqueville, *De la démocratie en Amérique*, Vol.3, Part 2, Ch. 2.
17. Cf., for example, the important recent book by A. Portelli, *L'ordine è già stato eseguito: Rome, le Fossé ardeatine, la memoria* (Rome, 1999).
18. Cf. M.A. Rivellia, *L'Arcivescovo del genocidio*: *Monsignor Stepinač, il Vaticano e la dittatura ustascia in Croaziai, 1941–1945* (Milan, 1998). I have not had the opportunity to see the volume recently published in the series Quaderni dell'Osservatore romano: G.P. Mattei, *Il Cardinale Stepinač: Una vita eroica nella testimonianza di quanti con lui sono satit vittime della persecuzione nella Jugoslavia comunista* (Rome, 1999).
19. The following quotations are taken from the *Jerusalem Post* (17 and 18 March 1998).

The Two Levels of Public Use of the Past

CLAUDIO PAVONE

The expression 'the public use of history' has entered common parlance since Habermas used it in his *Historikerstreit*. The development of the term as a critical tool in Italy is due mainly to Nicola Gallerano, who distinguished between the higher, scientific level of usage and a lower level which propagates the common understanding of history. This lower level, as he made clear, is not to be understood pejoratively; there is in fact a constant give and take between the two levels which creates a particularly interesting field of inquiry.[1] Moreover, it may actually be the professional historians themselves who allow the larger public to become familiar with their ideas, mainly through their more political writings. Renzo De Felice, for example, found himself in the midst of bitter historical and political polemics in Italy less because of the eight weighty volumes of his biography of Mussolini (written between 1965 and 1997) than because of the interviews he gave to newspapers and others published in slim polemical publications (1975 and 1995).[2]

The premise of the conference 'The Historian and Public Life', held at the Einaudi Foundation in Turin in November 1997, was that the demand that historians be active in public seemed to be intensifying, and it proposed examining 'the uses of the past in European and American public life'. The words 'political uses' are used again in the title of the current seminar, referring less to *history* than, in a broader sense, to the *past*.

A sense of the past and its ability to influence the present are in fact not confined to historiography; moreover, the public and political arenas make use not just of historiography but of other scholarly fields as well. Philosophy, religion, psychology, literature, anthropology, sociology, the figurative arts, archaeology, science, and culture of all kinds may be utilized for this purpose. It should perhaps be noted that this kind of use is less likely to arouse criticism when the humanities are involved. They are viewed, by their very nature, as being linked to the sociocultural and political context, in other words, to the historical situation, without this fact necessarily compromising the universal values that they embody. Scientific disciplines as well are now recognized as having their own historicity, but in order to protect their 'objective' character we tend only to think of their results, not their methods and the principles on which they are founded, as being available for practical and political use.

History occupies an intermediate position in this respect. A scientific and a literary nature – the latter understood as being the art of persuasion – coexist within historical writing. Quintilian, an ancient master of the art of oratory, wrote that 'historia est proxima poetis et quodammodo carmen solutum'.[3] Viewed in its scientific aspect, it is scandalous when history is bent to a political use; viewed in its broadly literary aspect, in contrast, it is simply expected, either implicitly or explicitly, that this should happen. People do become indignant, however, when history is taken over as an integral part of politics. The indignation is naturally all the greater when the political cause taking advantage of history is the opposing one.

Many arguments over the public use of history are, in my opinion, engendered by an unclear, perhaps deliberately obfuscated, distinction between the two aspects just mentioned. This distinction between the two levels of the public use of history derives from the general principles controlling the dual nature of historical knowledge. By separating them out it is possible to place the discourse in a more appropriate methodological framework.

The past lives on, first and foremost, in individual and collective memory. Marc Bloch has maintained that each generation has the right to record for the first time the events in which it has participated; he himself has given a clear example in his book on the 'strange defeat' that France suffered in 1940.[4] This means that the process of change from memory to history is very complex and not necessarily linked to the passage of time. Memory itself, both individual and collective, has a public use which may be compared with the public use of history. Le Goff, for example, is obviously aware of the problem of the relationship between professional historiography and the historical cultural media and of both of these with memory when he examines the relationship between history and memory in *Storia e memoria.*[5] Nora, for his part, emphasizes the importance of the divergences which may occur between individual and collective memory, adding that 'moins la mémoire est vécue collectivement, plus elle a besoin d'hommes particuliers qui se font eux-mêmes hommes mémoire': these exceptional persons, living repositories of memory, contribute to the public use of history, one should add, more on a popular than on a scholarly level.[6]

As the organizers of the conference pointed out, precisely at a time when historiography is undergoing a deep crisis of epistemology, the public use of history is conquering new realms. Le Goff has written that 'history has become an essential tool of the need for individual and collective identity'. This occurs in different ways depending on whether we are dealing with countries laden with an ancient national history which may by now be difficult to relate to, or with new countries 'concerned above all with providing themselves with a history' (Le Goff again), to bolster a national identity which is still in a raw state and of doubtful acceptance, at least on an international level.

Benedetto Croce coined the expression that all history is contemporary history, meaning by this that the problems impelling historical research can only be those endemic to the period in which the historian lives. The Italian scholar Adriano Tilgher wrote in 1928 that to avoid being crushed by the burden of the past, the new generation needed to make its own choice 'from the chaos of extinct centuries' of what would constitute its past.[7] There is no doubt that the public use of history draws deeply on this need, which draws it into a sometimes too casual mixing of the broad historiographical constructions and generalizations that are proposed.

The public use of history, in particular its political use, revives the ancient *querelle* about the relations between the judge and the historian. Here, as well, the debate is fed mainly by the confusions that arise on the second level of use. These confusions may even induce professional historians to express personal opinions on the issue, as Carlo Ginzburg has recently done in Italy.[8] Judges ought to heed the words of the evangelist: let your words be 'Yes, yes, no, no', all the rest is the work of the devil. In this sense, much of historical discourse is the work of the devil, because one of the historian's tasks is precisely to complicate things, pointing out nuances and contradictions, circumscribing the validity of judgements within recognizable limits. In some felicitous cases, the conclusions reached in juridical proceedings are the same as those arrived at by historiography; but, in general, judgements and other decisions arrived at in courts constitute merely one of the sources for history. Current use of history, richly fed by the second level, treats juridical proceedings as preferred resource material. This identification of court findings with facts may moreover be nourished by a strong need for substantial justice, which is directly identified with the justice of judges. Explicating this need and the misunderstanding underlying it becomes a task for historians, and other scholars of society.

The public use of history, on the first level, inspires explicit interdisciplinary efforts (which often, especially in Italy, exist more in word than in deed). Deep-rooted preconceptions deriving from historians' deepest convictions about life and the past and their visions of the future appear to be operating. On the one hand, historians are coauthors of what has been called 'the invention of tradition', on the other, generally when compelled to do so by great events, they take on the risky challenge of demythologizing it.

On the second level, attitudes towards the past are likewise conditioned by more recent events or, less consciously, by long term cultural structures. It may also happen that current use, precisely because it is closer to commonly held opinions, may enrich or call into question the overly intellectualized offerings of professional historians. This is why academics should not be too quick to condemn this second-level use of history but should confront it critically and analyze it in relation to the civil, cultural, and religious community in which it arises and obtains a hearing.

The two levels of public use of the past thus have deep common roots, and therefore analysts often pass from the first to the second. Professional historians find in this cause for simultaneous satisfaction and alarm. They are gratified to feel that they are socially useful, that they are participating in an effort at nation building (and sometimes Europe building and, in a future which is already upon us, 'Mediterranean building'), and addressing themselves to a much broader circle of consumers than they are accustomed to, but at the same time they fear that their intellectual and social independence might be compromised. Moreover, they have had limited ability, at least up to now and, again, mainly in Italy, to elaborate discourses which are simultaneously rigorous and compatible with modern techniques of mass communication. In the face of this difficulty, they often take refuge in disdain for the new forms of communication, particularly television. In reality, precisely because of the new technologies, often the second level increasingly influences the first. All this to some extent reduces the distance between the public use of history and scholarly historiography, both because of the entrepreneurship of those who manage the former and because of the lack of preparedness of scholars.

Lastly, we should not forget that there is also a public use for silence and oblivion. Renan, in his essay on the nation,[9] reminds us that oblivion is an integral part of constructing a national tradition and uses as an example the silence regarding the havoc created by the northern French in the south of France. Historians calling attention to facts like these are often criticized, but they too provide materials for the public use of history.

Some further distinctions need to be made at this point. The use of history has a 'diplomatic' level, an area of controversy (the old *bella diplomatica* or diplomatic war). The documents produced by chancelleries are full of them, and the broader public is particularly predisposed to absorb them and enlarge them, to the point of creating embarrassment for the consular officials themselves. The ideology of 'natural borders' is one of the most obvious examples in that it aims at transforming long term, complex historical processes into 'natural' phenomena. Lucien Febvre's *Le Rhin: Histoire, mythes et réalités* is a good example of the demystification of a classic and war-ravaged 'natural border'.[10] Italian irredentism claiming Trent and Trieste, which until 1918 were subject to Austria, made the Alps – according to nationalist rhetoric – the sacred border that God put at the top of Italy. Over the centuries, though, the Alps have served not only as an element of separation but also as one of civilized exchange between the peoples that inhabited their opposing slopes.

It is not only the state, and in particular the nation-state, that has a tendency to draw on the political use of the past. Local authorities may do this too. History provides abundant materials for municipal glory, most of them drawn from the second level of use insofar as they stem from a historiographical tradition preceding modern critical standards.

Churches, particularly the Catholic Church, have the same tendency. This age-old institution has turned history into apologetics, since it has bolstered revelation, as an argument based on faith, with tradition, that is, the history of the church. The *Acta Sanctorum* begun in 1643 by Bolland, the Jesuit, pursued, as Fueter reminds us, 'apologetic tendencies. They were trying to save the worship of saints from the attacks of Protestants and humanists by sacrificing to the extent necessary those legends which were most liable to provoke the ridicule of opponents'.[11] Blondel has clearly shown the impossibility of using history to support dogma;[12] it is the Bollandists who are, however, considered the founders of source criticism. The more they were assailed on the first level of public use of history, the more they served as supports for the second.

The great churches with universalistic pretensions, such as the Catholic and the Orthodox, have been able to nationalize their glories, making them integral parts of the national histories of some countries. Antonis Liakos has shown here how the Orthodox Church did this in Greece. During the Risorgimento, the Neo-Guelfs envisioned the pope as the future head of the projected federation of Italian states. The slogan 'La Roma onde Cristo è romano' (Rome, by which Christ is Roman) has long caressed the ears of Catholics, nationalists, and fascists and may still retain some of its seductive power.

Inscriptions, monuments, commemorations, and place and street names may be considered as lying halfway between the two levels of the public use of history. Inscriptions are often written in a courtly language recalling the stereotyped one that inspires medals for military valour. Few can manage to read them, however, at least in Italy, as they are often placed very high up on house walls. Their main value is a symbolic one, emphasized when they are removed because of changing times and political regimes. A similar argument may be made concerning place names. A proof is that in Italy, where Fascism was done away within a traumatic fashion, Fascist place and street names have been completely eliminated. In Spain, however, where the Franco regime exited smoothly and gradually, place and street names have remained largely unchanged.[13]

It is superfluous to dwell here on the importance of monuments as a vehicle of mass historical acculturation. The monument to Victor Emmanuel II stands out above all in Italy, overwhelming the Campidoglio next to it. Since it became the site of the tomb of the Unknown Soldier of

World War I, it has assumed the sacred name of the Altar of the Fatherland (this being the title of the recent book devoted to it by Bruno Tobia).[14]

Commemorations possess a courtly, solemn aspect and a popular aspect, which often takes on the form of a holiday. Pierre Nora's Collection *Les Lieux de la mémoire* speaks of an 'era of commemoration'. *La festa della nazione: Rappresentazione dello Stato e spazi sociali nell'Italia unita* is a fairly recent book by Ilaria Porciani,[15] while Cristina Cenci has contributed to a collection of essays entitled *Le memorie della Repubblica* with a study entitled 'Rituale e memoria: Le celebrazioni del 25 aprile' (the date of the liberation of Italy from Nazi and Fascist control in 1945).[16]

It is appropriate at this point to indicate some further particularities of the Italian case. Italy, which was unified in 1861, falls halfway between countries with an ancient and well consolidated national unity and those of more recent formation. The public use of the past as legitimation for the present has thus taken on particular characteristics. Italy has had to pass from a form of unity asserted only at the highest level, by intellectuals, to one that took on the form of the state and then had to be reaffirmed on a popular level. As the scholar Carlo Dionisotti has written, Italian culture 'has always been unifying and thus has transcended the actual divisions in the country and has possessed a meta-historical, idealizing character – in the language, in literature, and in political thought'.[17] It has not been easy to employ these universal characteristics as an instrument for nationalizing the masses of a country which is no longer able to recover its past splendour. Italians asked themselves during the Risorgimento why a unitary national state had not been constituted at the beginning of the modern age, and the discussion on this subject is not yet over.

During the Risorgimento, Abbot Vincenzo Gioberti claimed that Italians possessed a certain primacy in ethics and civilization, a primacy that the unitary state was unable to embody. The very interpretation of the meaning of the Risorgimento became a central theme, in a close intertwining of scholarly history and its public use. Both Fascism and the various currents of anti-Fascism tried to appropriate the Risorgimento, but 'difficulties in interpretation abounded, in this use of history, on both political sides'.[18] Among the anti-Fascists, who condemned Fascism as being anti-Risorgimento, there were frequent impulses to criticize the Risorgimento itself. The formula 'Second Risorgimento', used to designate the Resistance, is an example of the public use of a category which before being applied by historiographers was a political and civil description. 'Second Risorgimento' implied a strong current of ambiguity between a mere effort to defend the Risorgimento and a contradictory view of it as an incomplete and even misdirected process that finally had to be put back on the right path and brought to fulfilment.

One paradox in the public use of history in relation to national tradition lies in the fact that in the countries where this tradition is ancient and solid, history serves to confirm it and may even allow for a variety of internal interpretations which do not necessarily lead to political controversy. In countries which have recently acquired the form of nation-states, however, history is called in as an auxiliary for immediate and pragmatic public purposes. This provokes quarrels and pain when the pull in one direction of historical interpretation is countered by a pull in the opposite direction. Italy, as already stated, finds itself in an intermediate position, though this does not mean that the encounters are any less bitter. The contest takes place within a shared cultural vision and a willed rather than natural view of the nation, and this tends to intensify the confrontational attitudes of the opposing sides.

One should add that in Italy political history traditionally enjoys preeminence and that this also contributes to intensifying the antagonism among the diverse public uses of history. In the 1980s and 1990s, political history entered a crisis in the legitimation of politics and faith in the future. These parallel crises were due to various causes, not all of Italian origin, but they had the same foundation and in Italy tended to have the same results. The widening of the gap between research findings and pressure to justify current political trends with historical arguments is due to these crises. Historical arguments have been largely left to the second level of public use of history. The abandoning of values, much more than any contribution from research, has led to the spread of a false lack of prejudice that is reassuring in its oversimplification.

Furthermore, Italy continues to lack any tradition of historiography as narrative, in particular narrative with a view over the long term. The essayist style of Italian historiography (mainly historiography oriented to contemporary topics) at its best was able to draw on deep erudition and an ability to write well. Today's style, in contrast, encourages uninhibited ideological statements such as those mentioned above. This development has numerous consequences both for method and for quality.

Findings in social history, oral history, history that has contact with anthropology, the history of 'subjectivity', and other methodological innovations which have found an echo in Italy have received an uncertain transposition to the second level of the public use of history. There are few cases of findings in the new research fields' being used in public polemics. One case is that of work which, combining oral with traditional sources, highlights the conflicts and ambiguities in the memory of communities which suffered German and fascist massacres and reprisals between 1943 and 1945 (for example, the books of Battini, Contini, Forti, and Pezzino).[19] 'Contradictory memory' has been used as a tool for putting the two sides that were in conflict on the same level and even placing major responsibility on the side of the Resistance. The very consoling assertion has been derived from this that the sensible majority of the Italian people belonged to the so-called grey zone, aligning themselves with neither side.

In March 1997 an international colloquium was held in Aix-en-Provence entitled 'La Résistance et les Européens du Sud: La Pression de la conjoncture, les Poids de l'Histoire' (The Resistance and Southern Europeans: The Pressure of Circumstances, the Weight of History).[20] The colloquium's comparative viewpoint seems to me to be a precedent for the broader viewpoint of this seminar. It immediately raises two points which concern Italy again, since this is a European country which is both southern and Mediterranean, with rich relationships both with northern Europe and with the countries on the other shore of the Mediterranean.

In Italian historiography, Italy's distancing itself from Europe has always been viewed as one of the elements characterizing the country's decadence following the golden age of the Renaissance. One goal of the enlightened Italian elites has always been to rejoin the great modern European civilization to whose birth Italy made such an important contribution. The scholar and liberal politician Giustino Fortunato wrote sorrowfully in 1926, in the face of the triumph of Fascism, '[The Italians] are unequipped to advance at the same pace as the larger western European states, because as a result of the insubstantiality of Italy's political class they are condemned, like all Mediterranean peoples, to be at the mercy of events'. A scholar of a later generation, Costanzo Casucci, as late as 1960 admonished that ' Italy's fundamental problem from the Risorgimento until today has been that it is not a Portugal'.[21] Nationalism and Fascism both ignored this viewpoint and proclaimed Italy's primacy. These movements sought to turn Italian frustration *vis-à-vis* Europe into a conquering spirit directed not only towards the Balkans but towards East Africa and the other shore of the Mediterranean. In the Mediterranean Sea, Italy would win back ancient Rome's hegemony. Italy's claims to European territory (with the exception of Savoy, the cradle of the ruling dynasty) were all Mediterranean: Nice, Corsica, and Malta, defined in a Fascist song as 'the bulwark of the Roman spirit', and Dalmatia. Italian colonialism also had the characteristic of being a belated and senescent reaction to the French and British colonial empires: we were going into Africa to keep up with the other European powers.[22]

We Italians are well aware of the multiple historical resonances (in Libya they were also encouraged by archaeological excavations from Roman times) that nourished Fascism's imperialistic pretensions and those of the colonialism preceding it, but we are still discussing the extent to which these ambitions succeeded in creating a consensus. The Africanist Alessandro Triulzi has maintained that a broad-based colonialist consciousness was very insubstantial in Italy. In order to impose it, he wrote, the Fascists 'hammered the awareness of the Italians', creating symbolic imagery which was 'supposed to be capable of both neutralizing opposing internal positions – the other Italy, the Mezzogiorno – and distancing Italy from the external otherness – the colonial other – while recognizing in that other a dangerous proximity which had to be exorcized and transformed into difference'.[23] The south of Italy, in fact, has traditionally been viewed as a bridge to Africa, one which was to be crossed preferably in one direction only, north–south. And so the attitudes of northern Italians and southern Italians *vis-à-vis* colonial policy have often been different.

'Bizerte in the hands of the French is like a pistol pointing at Sicily' and 'Italy is breaking the chains holding it down in its sea' read the manifestos that were put up just before Italy entered the war in June 1940. The manifestos reflected the arguments of the nationalists, both the highest academics and the political militants, against the unwarlike and faint-hearted Little Italy of the liberals, which had allowed France to take Tunisia and in 1882 had turned down the British offer of a condominium over Egypt. The nationalist-Fascists, in order to find some historical support for expansion in the Balkans, emphasized Dalmatia's earlier Roman and later Venetian rule. Libya was, in fascist language, the 'fourth shore' (that is, after the Tyrrhenian, Adriatic, and Ionian coasts). Mussolini, astride a white horse and brandishing the sword of Islam in Libya, is the perfect symbol of an imperialism which was incapable of facing up to the problem of its political and cultural relations with the peoples of the other shore of the Mediterranean. In an imitation of the French *départements* of Algeria (the Latin and French Algeria about which Aymard has spoken at this conference), in 1939 the Fascist government declared that the four provinces created in Libya in 1934 were an integral part of metropolitan Italy. This was an administrative fiction of which no trace has remained in the memory of Italians or of Libyans. Wisely, the Italians shed few tears over losing the colonies after World War II, although today certain hotbeds of neo-nationalist revisionism call the indulgent peace treaty of 1947 a *diktat*.

After the war the public use of colonial history, which had taken refuge in the antiquated and too long surviving chairs of 'colonial history and politics', practically disappeared. This was because of the aforementioned lack of interest in and embarrassment about Italy's racist policy in the colonies, initiated before the racial laws covering metropolitan Italy were issued in 1938. Only the recent studies by Del Boca, Labanca, Rochat,[24] and

Triulzi and contacts with anthropological research have broken this silence, provoking bitter reactions on the part of the traditionalist historians who had appointed themselves custodians of what they called Italy's 'good reputation' in Africa.

The experience of World War II still constitutes a relevant field of comparative study in the Mediterranean area, fully involving both levels of the public use of history. South of the Mediterranean, new national states came into being in countries largely lacking democratic traditions. On the northern shore the existing states, having had such traditions in their past, were experiencing totalitarian regimes due to German and Italian occupation and indigenous antidemocratic tendencies. The field of collaboration with the occupiers is therefore a fruitful one for studying the confrontation between the two levels of public use of history in the various countries. In Italy, as in France, there was after the war an initial reaction of concealment of this phenomenon, which had disgraced the name of the nation. Nowadays, however, historiography asserts the need to analyze the experience of the war years in its totality. The use of critical tools appropriate for historical analysis – making distinctions in order better to interpret the phenomenon as a whole – is beginning to produce results, but they are often used on the second level to suggest an equivalence between the two once-opposed sides as the first step towards general reconciliation. This approach is entrusted with the task of eliminating the problem of responsibility *vis-à-vis* the past and providing a facile way of pacifying everyone's conscience. There seems to be a wish to extract the possibility of shared, civil coexistence from the dulling of conscience and historical memory. The practice, which in Italy is very widespread, of 'repenting' and asking pardon of a great variety of protagonists of historical events (for example, the Catholic Church's apology to Galileo Galilei) could be described as the tip of the iceberg of a new, shared sense of history which people are trying to diffuse. Echoes may be found in it of the confusion already mentioned of the judgement of history with juridical processes. Amnesty, a political and juridical event, thus becomes synonymous with the cancellation of memory and historical responsibility.

There is hardly any important problem in the recent history of Italy that has not been subjected in recent years to this double revisionist process: one process a physiological and healing one, which should produce its full results in the medium and long term, and the other a process which is rampant in the area of political publicity. This latter type of revisionism provokes both a defensive and unproductive guardedness on the part of traditionalists and obvious satisfaction on the part of those who have ties to the Fascist past and feel themselves finally vindicated and rehabilitated. What suffers is any growth in the country's civic conscience, which is in need of an accurate relation with the past and thus requires that the public use of history be conducted in a scholarly and rigorous way.

Fascism, its totalitarian character, the use of gas in Ethiopia, anti-Fascism, Italian anti-Semitism, the war, the behaviour of Italian troops in Balkan occupied territories, the Resistance, the violence following the insurrection, the behaviour of the Catholic Church (a subject which is treated with great care), the birth of the republic, the purge, the absence of any Italian Nuremberg, the Constitution of 1948, the continuity between the Fascist state and the republic, communism and the relation between its international dimension and Italian communism, black terrorism and red terrorism are at the centre of the public debate on both levels.

The discussion may have reached its greatest intensity, at least in open debate, in the dispute concerning the 'death of the fatherland' initiated by the very well known book by Ernesto Galli della Loggia bearing this title.[25] He argues that the defeat suffered by Fascist Italy in the war in which it was the ally of National Socialist Germany, a defeat sanctioned by the armistice of 8 September 1943, caused the collapse of Italian national identity itself. The resistance against the German occupiers and against the fascists who had returned to power in the form of the Italian Social Republic (the Salò Republic) was incapable of reviving it. The recent book by the well known journalist Silvio Bertoldi entitled *Apocalisse italiana: Fine di una nazione, settembre-ottobre 1943*[26] provides an example. All of Italian history, at least from the Risorgimento onward, has been invested in a debate in which the theme of identity and that of the very unity of the country have been confused. Scanning the contents of a recent volume by Denis Mack Smith, *La storia manipolata*,[27] one finds an inventory repertory, if an incomplete one, of the themes which have been the object of controversial public use, precisely from the Risorgimento onward.

Eric Hobsbawm, in an interview granted on the occasion of the conference, has said that in recent years 'the manipulation of history for ideological purposes has increased greatly' and added that even historians have been in some way responsible for this, with the result that 'it is their duty to find remedies': it is they in fact who provide materials for the manipulators.[28] In a recent essay of his on Primo Levi, Stuart Woolf has written that 'for Levi, the public use of memory was a moral and political act, which he shared with other survivor historians'.[29]

These observations by two authoritative British historians lead us to a final question: to whom do we answer for the public use of history and of memory, in other words of the past? The question is all the more difficult because contemporary historians' responsibility towards the past easily becomes a responsibility towards the future – or, rather, towards a history which is, in this case, still in the making. Historians, with their long term interpretations, which include the present, may appear to be making some assurances about the shape that the near future will assume. Anyone acting in a position of power obviously does take on greater and more obvious responsibilities. But, in contributing to creating the conditions inducing citizens to obey whoever is in command, historians have their own responsibility. This is not always an immediately political one, but its nature and importance within the framework of the general responsibility of the culture become clear. It is not true that 'inter arma non silent Musae' (among arms the Muses are not silent) (as went the title of a conference held in Warsaw in 1977); not even Clio remains silent a midst the clamour of war.

In April 1996, at the European University Institute in Fiesole, a conference was organized by the Società Italiana per lo Studio della Storia Contemporanea, the magazine *Passato e Presente,* and the European University Institute itself. The topic was 'The Contemporary Historian's Responsibility Today'. It clearly emerged that the contemporary historian has special responsibilities to society and to institutions beyond the professional and academic. The historian's responsibility derives from the role that society requires history to play and the likelihood that history will be put to public use. It is, moreover, the historical situation as a whole and what historians in performing their task determine is history that create this responsibility. One could therefore conclude by inviting historians to outline the history of public use of their own discipline so that it might become a full chapter in the history of historiography.

Translated by Judith Roumani

NOTES

1. N. Gallerano (ed.), *L'uso pubblico della storia* (Milan, 1995).
2. R. De Felice, *Intervista sul fascismo* (interview with M.A. Ledeen) (Rome and Bari, 1975); *Rosso e nero* (interview with P. Chessa) (Milan, 1995).
3. Cited in M. Stefanoni, 'Introduction', in Cornelius Tacitus, *Agricola, Germania, Dialogo sull'oratoria* (Milan, 1991), p.xxii.
4. M. Bloch, *L'étrange défaite* (Paris, 1957).
5. J. Le Goff, *Storia e memoria* (Turin, 1982), containing the entries written for the *Enciclopedia Einaudi.*
6. P. Nora, 'Entre mémoire et histoire: la problématique des lieux', in P. Nora (ed.), *Les lieux de la mémoire,* Vol. 1, *La République* (Paris, 1984), p.xxx.
7. Quoted by S. Woolf, 'Risorgimento e fascismo: il senso della continuità nella storiografia italiana', *Belfagor* 20 (1965), pp.71–91. See esp. p.84.
8. C. Ginzburg, *Il giudice e lo storico: Considerazioni in margine al processo Sofri* (Turin, 1991).
9. Ernest Renan, *Qu'est-ce qu'une nation?* (Paris, 1882).

10. L. Febvre, *Le Rhin: Histoire, mythes et réalités* (Ital. trans., Rome, 1998).
11. E. Fueter, *Storia della storiografia moderna* (Naples, 1943 [1911]), Vol. 1, p.389.
12. M. Blondel, *Storia e dogma* (Florence, n.d.); this contains the Italian translation of *Lettres sur les exigences de la pensée moderne en matière d'apologéthique* (1896) and *Histoire et dogme* (1904).
13. G. Ranzato, 'La storia della guerra civile nella Spagna postfranchista: uso e non uso', in Gallerano, *L'uso pubblico*, pp.135–44.
14. B. Tobia, *L'Altare della Patria* (Bologne, 1998).
15. I. Porciani, *La festa della nazione: Rappresentazione dello Stato e spazi sociali nell'Italia unita* (Bologne, 1997).
16. C. Cenci, 'Rituale e memoria: le celebrazioni del 25 aprile', in L. Paggi (ed.), *Le memorie della Repubblica* (Florence, 1999), pp.325–78.
17. C. Dionisotti, 'Intellettuali irresponsabili, avvicinatevi alla gente', interview by A. Riva, *Corriere della Sera* (Milan, 23 Feb. 1998).
18. Woolf, 'Risorgimento e fascismo', p.85.
19. M. Battini and P. Pezzino, *Guerra ai civili: Occupazione tedesca e politica del massacro, Toscana 1944* (Venice, 1997); G. Contini, *La memoria divisa* (Milan, 1997); C. Forti, *Il Caso Pardo Roques: Un eccidio del 1944 tra memoria e oblio* (Turin, 1998); P. Pezzino, *Anatomia di un massacro: Controversia sopra una strage tedesca* (Bologne, 1997).
20. J.M. Guillon and R. Mencherini (eds.), *UMR TELEMME, (Temps, Espaces, Langages, Europe Méridionale–Méditerranée), Colloquium, La Résistance et les Européens du Sud, 20–22 March 1997* (Paris, 1999).
21. Woolf, 'Risorgimento e fascismo', pp.77, 83.
22. See A. Del Boca, *Gli italiani in Libia*, 2 Vols. (Rome and Bari, 1986, 1988), and N. Labanca, 'L'Africa Italiana', in M. Isnenghi (ed.), *I luoghi della memoria: Simboli e miti dell'Italia unita* (Rome and Bari, 1996), pp.255–89.
23. A. Triulzi, 'La costruzione dell'immagine dell'Africa e degli africani nell'Italia coloniale', in A. Burgio (ed.), *Nel nome della razza: Il razzismo nella storia d'Italia* (Bologne, 1999), pp.165–81, quotation from pp.168–9.
24. A. Del Boca, 'L'Impero', in Isnenghi, *I luogi della memoria*, pp.417–37; N. Labanca, 'Il razzismo coloniale italiano', in Burgio, *Nel nome della razza*, pp.145–63; G. Rochat, *Il colonialismo italiano* (Turin, 1974).
25. E. Galli della Loggia, *La morte della patria: la crisi dell'idea di nazione tra Resistenza, antifascismo e Repubblica* (Rome and Bari, 1996).
26. S. Bertoldi, *Apocalisse italiana. Fine di una nazione, settembre–ottobre 1943* (Milan, 1998).
27. D. Mack Smith, *La storia manipolata* (Rome and Bari, 1998).
28. E. J. Hobsbawm, 'La Lega mistifica la storia', *Corriere del Mezzogiorno* (Naples, 29 Jan. 1999).
29. S. Woolf, 'Primo Levi's Sense of History', *Journal of Modern Italian Studies*, 3 (1998), pp.273–92.

Out of Place, Out of Time

ELIAS SANBAR

The contemporary history of the Palestinians turns on a key date: 1948. That year, a country and its people disappeared from both maps and dictionaries. The short war which raged from November 1947 to 15 May 1948 and terminated in the proclamation of the State of Israel, far from being a straightforward colonial occupation of one country by another, resulted in the replacement of one people by a community of 600,000 settlers transported to Palestine during the British Mandate. A universe disappeared, and of the 1,400,000 Palestinians in the country prior to the Nakba – 'the Catastrophe' – just 150,000 individuals were listed as being present during the first census carried out by the new Israeli state. 'The Palestinian people does not exist', said the new local masters, and henceforth the Palestinians would be referred to by general, conveniently vague terms, as either 'refugees', or in the case of the small minority that had managed to the escape generalized expulsion, 'Israeli Arabs'. A long absence was beginning.

Who were these men and women who from their world of camps and tents railed against the injustice inflicted on them? Were they really the nation they claimed to be? Did they have 'a country' prior to 1948? Were they aware of being a people – did they have a national identity – before they were driven onto the highways and byways of exile? Or were they, as the victors claimed, Arab 'nomads' who, after 'selling their lands' to the settlers, suddenly discovered a cause for themselves and proclaimed their national rights with the sole aim of 'driving the Jews into the sea'?

In order to address these questions, it is vital to have a number of reading 'keys', as well as a fairly free-ranging imagination. These two elements make it absolutely necessary to break out of the straitjacket – so dominant that today it seems a manifest truth – of the timeless, universal model. They compel rejection of the idea that any national identity necessarily involves the establishment of a nation-state in accordance with the modern transformations which have convulsed Europe since the eighteenth century. They require acceptance of the idea that a people can exist fully, with all that this implies in terms of national awareness, sovereignty, and the right to self-determination, despite not having a central and centralized state as a dominant and exclusive reference for its identity. This is not an easy approach to adopt, deviating as it does from a model which has spread far beyond the borders of the continent of its birth. It is also complicated by the fact that the Palestinian people, albeit born in novel conditions, now wish, like many other non-Western peoples, to establish a nation-state.

The Palestinians are predominantly Arabs from the Eastern Mediterranean. Since time immemorial their country has been part of what is called 'historical Syria', covering the regions which would later give rise to modern Syria, Lebanon, and Palestine. Their Arabness constitutes an underlying identity, a core which is common to the peoples of these regions. Binding factors include the use of the same language, the existence of a collective imagination, the claim of a shared history, and the reality of identical social structures. In other words – the same vision of the world, never refuted, insofar as local identity attributes bound up with particular region of this larger whole have for centuries constituted a centrifugal force which has linked and incorporated rather than excluding and dividing. Far from an idyllic multiple and harmonious world (internal and occasionally intercommunal conflicts do exist), we have here a form of society which has specifically allowed this common core to be enriched by its local variations, the outcome of a long period of maturation, which are like a set of variations on a theme.

These Arabs inhabit a particular land, Palestine, an Arab region that for centuries has borne a particular stamp and hence is the object of specific desires: Palestine is also the Holy Land, the cradle of monotheism, and its inhabitants consider themselves the 'People of the Holy Land'. They are not yet a people in the modern sense of the term, but they are already a community which considers itself the guardian of all the spiritual legacies for which it has been the cradle, a community which defines itself in terms of its own space and its own internal 'geography'. One of the consequences of this is an abiding pluralism which, although differing from 'democratic pluralism', enabled Palestinians to live with their community and local differences long before that term was coined.

This land has also, from Sumer and Pharaonic Egypt until World War I, been the obligatory route between the valleys of the Euphrates and the Nile. Any expansion out of one or other of these must necessarily traverse Palestine, and therefore the latter takes on an additional attribute: while it may constitute an inevitable corridor through which conquerors must pass, it is, however, practically never the ultimate target of conquests. Thus, over the centuries, Palestine would see the passing of reigns which, while they may have occupied the country 'while they were about it', nevertheless always had their eyes fixed elsewhere. As a result, it was better preserved than its neighbours, experiencing extended periods of tranquillity off the beaten track of history and its upheavals. This would also influence the identity of its inhabitants.

Paradoxically, the Crusades simply reinforced this state of affairs. By making the Holy Land their target – by singling out Palestine in this fashion and linking its deliverance from the infidels to the idea of redemption – the Christian armies of the West would highlight its specificity. Not until the nineteenth century and modern colonization would the Palestinians really participate in the upheavals generated by European expansion.

The Palestinian space which has been defined in these terms constitutes a human and geographical entity, a society which is largely identical with neighbouring Arab societies. One urban world, another which is rural and settled, and a third which is Bedouin, all characterized by an ascendancy of networks of clan and family ties, live and develop there. Jerusalem is the centre of this structure. But the holy city, albeit the country's chief political metropolis, the centre of its religious activities, and its symbolic focal point, is not its *sole* capital. This is not simply because Palestine is not yet a modern entity with a central seat of government but because its society is marked by substantial vertical splits, regional entities which also have their own 'capitals' – Haifa and Acre for the Galilee, Safed for the north near what is now Lebanon, Nablus for the central interior region, Al-Khalil Hebron for the southern interior region, Jaffa for the central coastal region, Gaza and Bi'r al-Sab' Beer-Sheva for the southern coastal area near Egypt. It is only Jerusalem, however, which has a dual role, being the centre of both the Jerusalem–Bethlehem region and the whole of Palestine.

This sociopolitical topography was to have decisive consequences for internal power structures, including the Palestine Liberation Organization, founded in 1964. Central power has been largely based on a confederation, and anyone desirous of leading this country and its people must win over its multiple regional components without tampering with their local powers. It is in this way that, through the dynamics of history and the sluggishness of locales, a society came into being which, for a very long time, has functioned in accordance with the principle of consensus and the search for a common denominator. In Palestine the 'national' has been constructed on the basis of respect for the aspirations of the 'local'.

It was this society which, in the nineteenth century, found itself involved in the general movement to cast off the yoke of the Ottoman empire and achieve sovereignty and independence. At the time, the dream was a pan-Arab one. The Palestinians, like their brothers and neighbours, aspired to a modern state, true, but a *unified* one, and the idea of the Arab nation – multihued and not exclusively Islamic as is constantly repeated in certain circles – was predominant. World War I put an end to this dream. Introducing the age of mandates, British or French, the modern borders of the colonial carving-up of territory grounded the principle of division in the land itself. For Palestine, which became the subject of a British promise to found a 'Jewish national home land' there, an additional dispossession was beginning. As Arthur Koestler put it, one nation had solemnly promised another the territory of a third. And in May 1911 the Palestinian reformist Sulayman al-Taji al-Farouqui issued the following premonitory warning, so amazing for a people which some say at that time had no awareness of its national identity: 'Zionism is the danger menacing our homeland ... It heralds our exile and our expulsion from our homes and our properties!'.

Although Palestinian identity was not born in 1948, nevertheless this year left its imprint on this people's national personality, as if its facial features had changed, or its voice had suddenly acquired a different resonance. From 1948 onwards the Palestinians occupied an alien territory. To call it 'exiled territory' is inadequate, for the Palestinians' displacement was in all matters constituting their identity rather than to alien lands. In 1948 the Palestinians were Arabs expelled to other Arab lands – those of peoples of which they saw themselves as an integral part – and if they were deprived of their country they were not by the same token 'dislocated'. The question, therefore is, what was the nature of this exile which would so profoundly shape their identity.

Having disappeared in 1948, Palestine left the stage. This was the visible part of the drama. Another part – invisible, underground – would take shape in the midst of the Palestinians, in their flesh, as it were. To escape the drowning, to rescue their land, which had been swallowed up, the refugees would gamble everything on taking it with them, gradually becoming the temporary replacement of their homeland. From now on, they would live as if they were everything – Palestine *and* Palestinians, a people *and* its land – while waiting for the latter to 'come home' and reoccupy its place on the map. An obsession with places, from general topography to the details of the tiniest street, would henceforth preoccupy them, with Palestine travelling around on the shoulders of its children.

By departing from space, the Palestinians, about whom the whole world agreed to say 'they do not exist', also departed from time. Their history and their past were denied. Their aspirations and their future were forbidden. Hence they found themselves trapped in an ephemeral dimension, and for half a century they would live in limbo, achieving a very special relationship with the concept of duration. Since the present was forbidden to them, they would occupy a temporal space made up of both a past preserved by a memory afflicted by madness and a dreamt-of future which aspired to restore time. And their obsession with places would be accompanied by a fervent desire to reestablish the normality of everyday lives.

Driven out of time and space, the Palestinians would ultimately see themselves as deprived of the right to their own name. Driven by an astonishing intuition – they knew that if the name were to be permanently obliterated, their disappearance would be confirmed – they would fight tooth and nail to preserve the existence of the words 'Palestine' and 'Palestinians'.

These three elements – land, which is transported, time, which is restored, and a name, which is preserved – constitute the ideology of the Return, and it is this ideology which constituted the basis of the national renaissance arising out of the exile. It has imparted its specific features to this Arab countenance of Palestine.

II

These briefly outlined features of the Palestinian national personality are of vital importance for addressing the question of the political uses of history. In the Palestinian situation, 1948 is a key date not only because of the tragic events which took place then but also because it marked the conclusion of a process of expulsion considered to substantiate a nation's disappearance. It will be understood, therefore, that from this date forth the perpetuation or disappearance of the people of Palestine; the new turn taken by the Israel–Palestinian conflict, the Israelis' need to establish that, since the Palestinians had never existed, no injustice to them could have been committed and the passion with which the Palestinians sought to prove that they had lost a homeland all contributed to an inordinate use of 'proof by History'.

In 1948 the Palestinians perceived their country not as occupied territory but as a land which had been swallowed up. The conflict took a radically new turn: henceforth, it would be a record of disappearances, not occupations. This is a crucial point. And the historian would, for the Palestinians, become an individual with a mission extending far beyond the field of research in the narrow sense. History, to the extent that it was deemed to guard against disappearance, became an 'emergency science'.

History was thus called upon for help in legitimizing the aspirations of one camp or the other. Such use is certainly not exclusive to the Israeli–Palestinian question. but here – insofar as one of the two parties was obsessed by the idea of restoring historical 'time', while the other was terrified by the idea that this restoration would be accomplished only at the price of its own exit from that 'time' – it became imbued with inordinate intensity. From 1948 onwards, each of the two protagonists viewed its history as excluding that of the other. Beyond this, precedence in terms of presence in the land amounted to an *exclusive and unshared* right to be present in that land. In other words, it legitimized not only one party's current existence but also the *absence* of the other.

Until 1948, the dominant mode of writing history among the Palestinians was that of chronicles, and the few works that are presented as 'modern historical works' are, in fact, simply textbooks. As pointed out elsewhere,[1] practically all historical writings took the form of individual diaries. The Arab cause in Palestine was of course at the centre of this work, but the viewpoint was that of the chronicler's clan region. The very specific information that these chronicler-historians provided was something that they had themselves experienced and recorded.

The 1948 expulsion was marked by an impressive piece of writing, the first of its genre, entitled *Al-Nakba* (The Disaster), by 'Arif al-'Arif,[2] which was not just a detailed chronicle of 1948 but a rather comprehensive compilation of all the particulars, factual and other, of the event. This chronicle not only addressed a subject on a national scale but was based on all the clan regions of the Palestinian nation. It was at once the culmination of the chronicle form and the beginning of its disappearance.

From now on, history would be developed by Palestine's refugee historians in accordance with three new approaches:

1. The catalogue. Born of the profound trauma caused by the loss of a world and immersed in the idea of the Return, the catalogue seeks to list everything that has disappeared. Containing biographies interspersed with descriptions of people and places, it has a dual purpose: to rescue from oblivion a land which will from now on be invisible and, by drawing up a genealogy of places, to prove the precedence of the Palestinian presence.
2. The plot. Here the intention is to show that the homeland was lost because of a conspiracy of the Great Powers and the treason of the Arab regimes which 'sold out' to them. Hence the works which appeared in great numbers from the 1950s onward were in perfect symbiosis with the events which were shaking the Arab world at the time and with Nasserism.
3. University-based modernism. This is the work of the generation of Palestinians that, from the 1940s onward, attended European – particularly British – universities before going on to study or teach at the American University of Beirut in the 1950s. Under the leadership of Constantin Zurayk – a modernist, secular Syrian historian and the author of *Ma'na al-Nakba* (The Keys of the Nakba), a seminal work which for the first time asked the rational questions about the loss of Palestine and called for the drawing of lessons from history – Palestinian historians began to draw inspiration from two premises. Palestine was lost because

the Arabs had not entered modernity, and the solution was to combine modernity and Arabness. The PLO intelligentsia were to emerge from this trend.

These three trends coexisted for a number of years before the university approach, conveyed through the revived of the national movement in exile, emerged dominant. This ushered in a new phase marked by the central – perhaps exaggerated – place occupied by the *historian*. A symbolic figure combining knowledge with commitment in the vanguard of the 'scientific and national struggle', the historian was seen as capable of drawing lessons from history, safeguarding the past denied by Israel, and above all providing the proof and the scholarly arguments needed to establish the accuracy and legitimacy of aspirations.

III

Today, driven by the peace negotiations, a new reality is emerging among historians. Now that Palestine has 'regained its place', a tendency towards 'normalization' can be identified, as if, released from political responsibilities, historians – without abandoning their commitment (the negotiations are far from over) – could do their work without becoming involved in defending the subject. In other words, it is finally possible to drop the defensive approach, to enjoy the luxury of 'forgetting' Israel for a moment in order to look, for example, at Palestine's medieval or Ottoman history and at the day-to-day life of its people, as well as expanding the field of study to include spheres external to Palestine without being forced to address them in terms of their relation to the Arab–Israeli conflict.

It is in the light of this new state of affairs that historians – whether well-established figures such as Walid Khalidi or younger colleagues such as Yazid Sayigh – have begun publishing innovative studies of their country's contemporary history and, more specifically, of the history of resistance and the national movement. In a sense this trend is the Palestinian equivalent of what in Israel is called the 'new history' and for a number of years has involved rereading and questioning the dominant Israeli account of the events of 1948.

In parallel, although not part of history in the strictest sense, a vital development is appearing in fiction in the form of works whose material is based on tales of the Nakba. Paradoxical though it may seem, as long as their exile remained absolute the Palestinians said practically nothing about the exodus – only about its consequences. It is as if the trauma they experienced had made them mute, as if absolute absence has banned tales about its beginnings until the *return to the land had begun*. These novels –

such as Faysal Hourani's five-volume epic,[3] which draws its material from eyewitness testimony – are a first in the history of Palestinian literature. Apart from their literary calibre, they constitute an extremely rich source for the historian and are a sure sign of profound change. With them, life is bursting into print.

Translated by Ruth Morris

NOTES

1. Elias Sanbar, 'Le vécu et l'écrit: Historiens-réfugiés de Palestine', *Revue d'études palestiniennes*, 1 (1981).
2. 'Arif al-'Arif, *Al-Nakba*, 6 Vols. (Beirut and Saida, 1956–60).
3. Faysal Hourani, *Roads of Exile*, 5 Vols. (Damascus and Ramallah, 1994–2001).

Political Uses of History in Spain

PEDRO RUIZ TORRES

Politics has always been closely bound up with history, which in turn has often been used for political purposes.[1] History is currently playing an important political role in many different societies. Where the shaping of a national identity remains a problem or where old conflicts still linger, setting peoples or nations against one another, it occupies the centre of political debate and serves to justify a wide variety of actions and opinions. But even where there are no such problems, history is strengthening its ties with politics. Historians, or at least some of them, are beginning to become known for their repeated appearance in the media when it comes to matters of internal or international politics. A considerable number of history books and memoirs and publications of a popularizing nature reveal clear political motivation, not to mention the debates that they provoke. But it is undoubtedly in commemorations that the increasing politicization of history is seen most clearly. Historical commemorations sponsored by a wide range of governments follow hard on each other's heels.

In Spain, 1998 was the year of commemorations *par excellence*, just as 1995 had been in the countries that celebrated the fiftieth anniversary of the end of World War II. Spain had not taken part in that war – although the then recently established dictatorship of Franco had shown that it favoured Nazi Germany and Mussolini's regime – and was therefore in no position to recall the defeat of fascism, but in 1998 it was faced with a very special occasion. Several commemorations coincided that year. The first was the centenary of Spain's military defeat at the hands of the United States in the Spanish–American War, which brought about the loss of the last remnants of the colonial empire in America and the Pacific islands. In 1898 that empire disappeared completely, plunging Spain into a 'decline' against which a reaction came from a group of intellectuals – the so-called Generation of '98 – who were highly critical of the political system of the monarchy of the time. This was in a way an awkward, inopportune commemoration for the current rulers, but in the same year another commemoration came to their aid: the quarter centenary of the end of the extremely long reign of Philip II, the king who raised the Spanish empire to its highest point in Europe and America. Also in 1998, the democratic constitution that governs the current political system celebrated its twentieth anniversary, something without precedent in the entire history of Spain.

These are not the only historical dates to have been specially commemorated in Spain during the past decade. Going back to the Socialist period, in 1988 there was the celebration of the bicentenary of the death of Charles III, a moment used for official exaltation of the reformist work of the very moderate enlightened Spaniards, contrasting with the slight interest aroused a year later by the bicentenary of the French Revolution. In the same year, 1988, the nationalist autonomous government of Catalonia promoted the celebration of the 'millennium of the Catalan nation', and in 1992 it placed special emphasis on the centenary of the *Bases de Manresa*, represented as the origin of modern political Catalanism. None of those events came anywhere near achieving the impact of the great commemoration *par excellence*, the quincentenary of the 'discovery' of America, promoted in this case by the national government at the height of the Socialist era. In the 1990s there were also commemorations of less substance and without much official support which did not penetrate deeply into public opinion but served to recall, for example, the figure of the dictator Franco 100 years after his birth (1992), and the completion of 20 years since the beginning of the transition to democracy (1995) and 60 years since the start of the Civil War (1996). In 1997, with the right-wing government of the Popular Party having recently assumed power, official interest in historical commemorations became apparent once again. The reason that year was the centenary of the assassination of the Conservative leader Antonio Cánovas del Castillo, the architect in 1874 of the restoration of the monarchy and the consolidation in Spain of a moderately liberal parliamentary regime that, nevertheless, subsequently proved incapable of evolving towards true democracy. Immediately afterwards came 1998, as noted, and the commemoration of the 100 years since the colonial 'disaster' and 400 years since Philip II's death.

The commemorations just mentioned are examples of a new kind of political use of history. Today the myths cultivated by national/Catholic fundamentalism have become things of the past, as has the ideological combat that conditioned the development of Spanish historiography for most of the twentieth century. The *new political uses of history* are of a different kind. Most often they have the support of historians and an academic backing that makes them professionally 'respectable'. Criticisms of the motivation for these institutional initiatives rarely achieve public notice. The installation of democracy led to a weakening of the old myths and great ideologies against the background of which a tradition of 'scientific history' had laboriously been created. Politically committed academic activity began to be abandoned, and most professional historians attached a high value to the cultivation of aseptic monographs and professional debate among specialists as natural elements of their work. In many cases this attitude then became compatible with an evident sense of pleasure in initiatives of an institutional nature that presented the appearance of 'scientific professionalism'. The social impact of these initiatives conferred on history a usefulness all the more appreciable as the weight of the old discipline in our current educational system diminished. At the same time, history increasingly became a target of political exploitation, although in a new way.

The *politics of history* in Spain at present cannot simply be reduced to the country's intense involvement in official commemorations during the past decade. In a quite different context we must also refer to the role played by legal proceedings of international scope such as those that elucidated the participation of Franco's government and certain Spaniards close to it in the plundering of Jews during World War II, or magistrate Baltasar Garzón's action against Pinochet for his responsibility in connection with the torture and murder of Spanish citizens, among others, in Chile after the military coup against Salvador Allende's democratic government. There has also been a very significant response in the media to certain polemics, such as those focusing on the nature of the Franco regime and its similarities and differences with respect to fascism,[2] the pros and cons of a transition not as exemplary as we had been led to believe,[3] and, recently, the controversy over the role of certain outstanding intellectuals in the 1940s, supporters of the dictatorship at the time and later outstanding points of reference in the opposition to it.[4] The educational function of history has become the subject of intense political debate,[5] and two university events have evoked politically uncomfortable memories: the reception and tribute given to survivors of the International Brigades in the auditorium of the University of Valencia and the conference on the *Maquis* (the Republican guerrilla forces that continued armed resistance against Franco's dictatorship after the end of the Civil War) also organized within that university.

The political role currently played by history in Spain is not comparable to the part it played in the time of Franco's dictatorship, but equally it contrasts with the silence and forgetfulness promoted during the transition to democracy *by political means* (parties, government) and *for political purposes* (to help to bring about a peaceful transition from dictatorship to democracy after Franco's death in 1975). The desire to achieve a peaceful solution supported by a broad consensus made certain questions about the past awkward. The political climate of the late 1970s and early 1980s tended to favour forgetfulness with the aim of encouraging concord and reconciliation among Spaniards. The transition to democracy was accompanied by fear of remembering the immediate past; the future counted more than a history full of failures which some might use as weapons against others. Directly or indirectly, the great catastrophe of the Civil War continued to weigh upon the conscience of most Spaniards. However, as democracy became established and the intensity of the changes turned Spaniards away from fratricidal conflict and as those who had lived through the Civil War moved out of the public eye or disappeared, the amnesia ceased to have the political meaning conferred upon it by the 'agreed-upon' transition to democracy. In the new atmosphere of the late 1990s we begin to see signs of a personal and collective need to recover the past in a different way, far removed from the commonplaces promoted by the old ideologies and from the oblivion that falsely closed the wounds of the past during the transition.

THE POLITICS OF HISTORY AND NATIONAL IDENTITY

Of all collective identities, national identity is by far the one that has predominated in the past two centuries. A certain tradition of memory and history crystallized around the nation as a new hegemonic collective identity. The France of the Third Republic is the supreme example of the process of constructing a tradition of memory (*les lieux de mémoire*) and a science of history that remained in the hands of professionals specialized in its study and convinced that they were employing the 'scientific method' and had the ability to convert documents into 'objective evidence' derived from the past. The use of that tradition of memory and science of history for political ends (to legitimize, unite, and perpetuate the nation-state) and the close link between it and nationalist ideology have been pointed out on numerous occasions. However, there are other aspects of the relationship between politics, memory, and history that deserve to be taken into consideration and that arise only when the frame of reference is not the process of building a strong hegemonic national identity at the prompting of the state, in the style of France, but the manifest weakness of the state when that objective has been achieved.

Spain is different from other Mediterranean countries in a number of ways. The use of history has also played a fundamental political role here in ideological conflicts, especially in the conflict that arises from the construction of a 'state-centred' national identity. At the heart of that process and with that conflict as a setting, memory and history have been used in an uncritical, simplistic way for purposes of ideological propaganda. In Spain as in France and Portugal, the modern state goes back to a very early date, and therefore in the origins of this state both history and politics were subordinated to the interests of certain social sectors and corporations with their particular privileges. The modern state arose in Spain, as in France and Portugal, long before the existence of a public sphere favourable for the exercise of politics as we understand it now or of a specific professional environment for the cultivation of history. It was, therefore, a state that preceded nationalist ideology, a state that over several centuries acquired modern features which did not, however, include considering the imposition of a national identity. What is characteristic of Spain, however, is that the state sought to legitimize itself through an ideology, that of the Catholic empire, which, while not yet strictly nationalist, was later able to evolve towards a kind of nationalism that has left a long, deep mark on our contemporary history.

Two further characteristics are provided by the fact that during the period of nationalisms Spain, in contrast to France, lacked a strong, incontrovertible national identity and a history to support it in a professional, 'scientific' way.[6] Throughout the twentieth century the weak establishment in Spain of that identity and that type of history was linked with the emergence of two kinds of conflict: conflict between various conceptions of Spanish national identity, which prevented the development of a hegemonic national consciousness, and conflict between those who supported a Spanish identity and those within the state who rejected that identity and defended the constructions of national identities other than the Spanish. These conflicting identities created their own images of the past and advocated different kinds of history.

As a result, no strong hegemonic tradition of a nation-state variety of memory/history emerged in Spain. History that identifies nation with state and provides them with a common nation-state-centred identity recognized as belonging to them by most citizens – the 'classical' or 'traditional' history capable of forming or reinforcing a national consciousness that coincides with the territorial limits of the state – has had little social influence. Still less, therefore, have there been the conditions necessary for using that memory/history to create a national critical history, the kind of history that Pierre Nora has proposed in France, starting from the concept of *lieux de mémoire*[7] and seeking to adapt national history to the new scientific and civic needs of our time. The odd study on 'places of memory' can be found in Spain,[8] but the country lacks a tradition capable of establishing itself in the academic world and in public opinion in such a way as either to maintain interest in a traditional kind of national history or to propose a new national history setting out from the alternative proposal of *lieux de mémoire*.

That there is no strong hegemonic tradition of a nation-state variety of memory/history in Spain at present can be verified in three ways. First, during the past three decades the history of Spain has gradually been displaced by history concerned with subjects other than the nation-state such as stateless nations and regions (the 'autonomous communities'), small societies of a local nature (rural or urban), or social groups (social classes, professional groups, women). The recent reaction to this abandonment of the history of Spain is eloquent in this connection. Some recently published histories of Spain (those of García de Cortázar and Tusell)[9] must be placed in this context, but their relative success in publishing terms must by no means be understood as a trend. Second, the recent 'debate on the humanities' has highlighted a profound divergence among the various public authorities with responsibilities for education (central government and autonomous governments), between public authorities and historians, and even among historians.[10] This conflict, which has attracted public attention, is indicative of the current complete lack of agreement about the kind of history that should be taught in Spain.

Third, there is the polemic nurtured by the various party leaders and certain groups of intellectuals with a strong influence on public opinion – because of their frequent appearances in the media – about whether the democratic state is authorized to promote a nationalization of collective memory and of history. The fact that there is discussion about whether such a nationalization makes sense nowadays and how it should be carried out (whether in favour of a predominantly Spanish national identity or of recognition of the various national identities on an equal footing, where the plurality of national entities should lead, and so on) shows a total lack of political consensus. On the one hand there are those who support reinforcing Spanish national identity and for that purpose recovering the history of Spain while at the same time promoting the nationalization of memory and history as classically conceived. On the other hand, there are those who reject the idea that the 'state of autonomous regions' should even consider such a possibility, since it would favour the cultural and political standardization characteristic of the past in the face of the tendency towards plurality and decentralization of our time. The former complain of the absence of a memory and history of the Spanish nation that might provide a solid basis for awareness of a common identity extending to all inhabitants of the state. The latter criticize the attempt to use history to legitimize state-centred nationalism and advocate the creation of new collective identities, both supranational (a united Europe) and subnational (cities, regions, former stateless nations).

To use a musical metaphor borrowed from Jeffrey Olick,[11] it seems as if, after a long period during which the *homophony* of the eschatology of the church persisted, only relatively recently to disappear, modern Spain has fully entered the *polytonality* of multiculturalism without having known, other than briefly and always imperfectly and controversially, *the polyphony* of national state ownership.[12]

TWO POLITICALLY OPPOSED KINDS OF HISTORY

The fact that Spain lacks a strong, deeply rooted tradition of memory/history of the kind that we find in nation-states in the West is clearly due to a variety of factors that could equally account for the much discussed weakness of the nation/state in our country.[13] As far as the constitution of that tradition is directly concerned, in twentieth century Spain there were two almost opposite ways of representing the past and the *process* or path traced in it.[14] Those two conflicting global views of our history were nourished by the clash between two ideologies that disputed political hegemony throughout the nineteenth century and the better part of the twentieth. The deep ideological and political fracture of Spain that gave rise to those two traditions of historical memory goes back to the point when the *ancien régime* went into a crisis and the liberal revolution made its appearance. Since then the conflict, sometimes latent and sometimes manifest in the form of successive civil wars, has been reproduced equally in the view of the past and in the use of history as a basis for national identities in the new state. Two opposed views of the history of Spain – one here called 'orthodox' because of its traditional nature and another in tune with liberal thinking – confronted one another without either managing to achieve clear dominion for most of the twentieth century.

The 'orthodox' view has its roots in the religious and state-centred conception that emerged at the time of the Catholic empire, when the Spanish monarchy expanded in Europe and created a huge colonial empire in America. This conception of history had the implicit consent of the new state, which, despite its formally liberal nature, left primary education in the hands of the Catholic Church. Later, during the twentieth century, 'orthodox' history had the support of two dictatorships (the dictatorship of Primo de Rivera, between 1923 and 1930, and the dictatorship of Franco, between 1939 and 1975, the latter with totalitarian pretensions), and it was very much present in schools until at least the 1960s.

The 'orthodox' history of Spain is a simple Manichean account of historical events enacted by heroes and martyrs of the national/Catholic cause. Without a break, the thread of that history links the prehistoric origins of the 'beloved country' (the moment when the Celtiberians, with their 'simple customs' and 'independent nature', brought about the emergence of the 'true Spanish race') to the 'miracle' of the introduction of Christianity (thanks to St James the Apostle and the intervention of the Virgin of the Pillar), the constitution of the Visigothic Catholic monarchy (which united the Peninsula for the first time), and the advance of the Reconquest during the Middle Ages (which finally succeeded in expelling the invaders who supported the 'false prophet Mohammed'). Seen in this way, the history of Spain culminates in the glorious reign of the Catholic monarchs with the definitive religious and political unification of the country, the creation of the 'Holy Tribunal of the Inquisition', which succeeded in preserving national/Catholic unity, and the 'discovery' of America, opening up the new continent to Hispanic evangelization. Later there is the pinnacle of the Christian empire during the reigns of Charles V and Philip II and the increasing decline as rulers moved away from the designs of divine providence, gave up the traditional spirituality promoted by the Catholic Church, and fell into the hands of 'materialistic and foreign' ideologies alien to the 'true nature' – spiritual and national – of the Spanish people.

This interpretation of history, which set out to explain the greatness and decline of Spain in accordance with its adherence to church and monarchy, preserved a distinctly traditional, antimodern character derived from the old counter-Reformation ideology from the time of the empire. With a few significant modifications it was able to adapt to the new middle-class society and (especially in the rural Spain that continued to predominate until the mid-nineteenth century) counteract the political advances of liberalism. Thanks to the predominant role of the Catholic Church in primary education, this kind of history was very much a part of the education of Spaniards until the last third of the twentieth century.[15]

Later, the Franco regime used the national/Catholic view of the history of Spain and the tradition of memory that it provided (St James the Apostle, Covadonga and Pelayo, el Cid, the Catholic Monarchs, *Hispanidad*) to legitimize a national/militarist ideology and a theocratic/charismatic conception of the state that was fittingly personified by the figure of the Caudillo or 'Leader'. The Caudillo, having won the war, thereby became the one chosen by divine providence to rescue Spain from its decline and lead it along the path to the imperial glory of bygone years. In this way, with the sole but important modification that militarist *caudillismo* introduced in occupying the position of the monarchy, vacant since the victory of the Second Republic, during Franco's era the history of Spain officially continued to correspond to the same divine plan that had long before been 'revealed' by national/Catholic ideology and historiography.

According to this view of the past, the Spanish people, who had been chosen by divine providence, constantly displayed a national character in harmony with the spiritual values of the Catholic Church, values of which the army, triumphant in the Civil War of 1936–39, was now the main guarantor. All this provided a basis for the indissoluble unity of Spain and gave meaning to the struggle against any kind of 'invasion, heresy, separatist tendency and pernicious lay ideology, anti-Spanish by nature', among which freemasonry, liberalism, and communism were prominent. When Spain had good rulers whose desire was not to imitate other nations but 'to maintain the virtues of the race' and 'to follow the designs of God', it attained its 'supreme imperial greatness'.[16]

This religious fundamentalist conception of the history of Spain obviously had an ideological basis with traditional, antimodern leanings that its promoters at no point sought to hide. With such an ideology there was little need for the research work of professional historians, work that at the beginning of the twentieth century was barely established academically in Spain, in contrast to France or Germany, and that hardly began to be developed during the first third of that century. For the national/Catholic representation of the past to adorn itself with a certain intellectual air it was sufficient to refer to the work of prestigious Catholic philosophers of the nineteenth century such as Donoso Cortés y Balmes or to fall back on the most reactionary ideas of the early Menéndez y Pelayo.

To combat such a view of the past it was not sufficient for a different kind of history to emerge in the academic world. It was undoubtedly important that in some classes in secondary education institutes and universities at the end of the nineteenth century a history appeared that was conceived as a positive science ready to dismantle reactionary myths and criticize the manipulation of the past. But challenging the traditional ideology required an alternative global view, and for this purpose, in addition to the scientific conception of history, literature with a historical content and especially the new literary genre of the historical novel proved enormously useful.[17]

The liberal view of the history of Spain was much more in accord with the modern nationalist spirit that was developing in the more advanced states in Europe, but it was limited with regard to its development in universities and its diffusion in society. Following the lines of liberal ideology, the course of history now became a permanent setting for the struggle of the Spanish people against political or religious tyranny. Without relinquishing the idea of the very ancient origins of the Spanish nation, liberal criticism focused on the end of the Visigothic monarchy (because it was a theocratic one) and the times of religious intolerance, especially during the era of Philip II. The Middle Ages were positively evaluated in terms of the limitations on monarchic power imposed by the Spanish parliament and municipalities in the Christian kingdoms and the religious tolerance that, despite the war, existed on both sides during the Reconquest. The particular characteristic of Spain, it was even said, was the coexistence of Christians, Moors, and Jews in the Middle Ages, despite the conflicts that it caused. In modern times there was a special attraction in attempts to set limits to authoritarian power, as happened during the revolts of the *Comunidades* in Castile and the *Germanías* in Valencia. The enlightened reformism of Charles III's reign, in the mid-eighteenth century, was presented as the beginning of a truly Spanish revolution, subsequently cut short by the shameful reign of Charles IV and the Napoleonic invasion.

After a nineteenth century of constant civil wars and conflicts that prevented the occurrence of the revolution that the country needed, a new stage seemed to commence at the start of the twentieth century with prospects of the 'regeneration' of Spain. The material and intellectual progress of the Spanish people depended on the success of that revolution, which quite clearly was to be one promoted from above and aided by the enlightened classes, thus avoiding the violent outbreak of mass discontent that was perceived as an imminent danger. This view of history was bound up with a plan of transformation that set its sight on modern developed Europe and considered the old traditional Spain, the Spain that officially professed to be Catholic, an encumbrance from the past. Similarly, in the opinion of the more advanced liberals, political unity could be preserved only by the concession of a greater degree of freedom, so that the different peoples of which Spain consisted could be provided with their own governments (either from a radical perspective, disposed to refound the state, as defended by republican federalists with scant success, or else from a different perspective, much more moderate in tone and autonomist and regionalist in style). It was a further lesson provided by the liberal, lay, progressive history that in different periods of our development a common popular democratic demand for decentralization and self-government resisted the repression exercised by authoritarian powers.

This liberal, nationalist conception of the history of Spain, contrasting with the tradition of memory promoted by the national-Catholic view, had its moment of victory, albeit short-lived, during the Second Republic (in the historiographic renovation whose most outstanding figure was Rafael Altamira).[18] Subsequently, from 1939 onwards, it had to seek refuge in exile or in secrecy as the winners of the war imposed an almost complete disregard of those ideas until Franco's dictatorship began to tolerate a certain sort of dissidence in the late 1950s.

THE END OF THE DICTATORSHIP AND THE TRANSITION TO DEMOCRACY

In the final stage of the dictatorship the out-and-out supporters of the Franco regime continued, with more or less scholarly rigour according to their level of education and intellectual stature, to defend a traditional, 'orthodox' history of Spain, repeating the clichés of *hispanidad* and identification with Catholicism, the unity of the nation since remote times, the Christian empire that had been succeeded by a decline due to bad rulers, and criticism of the enlightened reformism, liberalism, and socialism that had been imported from abroad. In addition to all this there was now a special interest in the figure of Ferdinand VII, the king who, between 1815 and 1833, sought to preserve the traditional order characteristic of the *ancien régime* and introduce certain economic reforms. After his death, which some saw as a forewarning of what would happen when Franco disappeared, the crisis of the *ancien régime* – according to this reactionary view of our history – gave way to a chaotic nineteenth century of interminable fratricidal fights with no strong power capable of containing them, an image of the imminent disaster foreseen by those who supported the dictatorship at all costs. Those who opposed the regime, in contrast within a very broad ideological spectrum, resisted the image of a Spain historically incapable of freedom and democracy and the idea of a Spanish character inherently opposed to the modern values prevailing in Europe.

It is not a question here of analysing in detail how the traditional view of the history of Spain lost credibility and the capacity for political legitimation in the final years of Franco's dictatorship. Various factors contributed, among them (a) the social effects of the accelerated industrialization and urbanization of the 1960s; (b) the changes that took place within the Catholic Church as a result of the Second Vatican Council; (c) the opening up to Europe that the dictatorship allowed with a view to its own perpetuation; (d) the work of a generation of new historians in Spain who undertook the task of demolishing the official orthodoxy and provided a totally different interpretation, from a liberal perspective but adopting the new economic and social history that prevailed in Europe at the time; and (e) access to secondary and university education for an ever greater proportion of the population. All of these things helped to weaken a strongly ideologized representation of the past, the simple Manichean view of our history described as 'orthodox' which, during much of the twentieth century, shaped the mentality of a large number of Spaniards. Nowadays this view of the past is so remote and foreign that it is almost a curiosity; hence its appeal for readers or audiences when it is shown to us in books, films, or plays about those times.[19] However, mentalities and attitudes shaped by this 'orthodox' view of the history of Spain are still much more prevalent in Spain than is generally believed.

As society became industrialized during the 1960s and an increasing number of young people gained access to secondary and higher education in Spain, history began to develop as a discipline in our universities, as had happened in other nearby countries long before. At the time, during the 1960s and early 1970s , that is to say, at the height of the struggle against the dictatorship, that development did not exclude political commitment on the part of some historians. A fair number of them made this quite clear without there being any effect on the quality of the research that they conducted. Thanks to the impressive advance that took place in historical research during those two decades, it was possible to write the history of Spain from a perspective previously unknown and in a totally new way, less national and Spanish-centred, broader and more varied than had been imagined by classical liberal progressivism, and without the old organicist essentialism that had previously permeated the liberal view of the past.[20]

The history subsequently produced in Spain took its place fully within the framework of renovation, sharing its multiplication of subjects of investigation, exploration of new sources, and use of new methods which in general terms led to a division of historiography into separate subdisciplines. The absence of great debates was the most striking feature in the case of Spain, accompanied by an accumulation of publications about the most diverse topics but without major works of synthesis such as those that had appeared at the beginning of the process of transformation. The new 'state of autonomies' favoured a separate history for each of the regions or nationalities that constituted Spain. For these and other reasons, the victory of democracy did not resolve the old conflict between the two nationalist ideologies and their respective views of the past in favour of the constitution of a single tradition of Spanish national memory/history. On the contrary, democracy made the disagreement even plainer.

Nevertheless, in a political context that changed radically as the transition to democracy took place, general views about the history of Spain underwent very significant modifications. In the early stages of the historiographic renovation, during the 1950s and 1960s, the period that aroused the interest of historians was the time of transition from the *ancien régime* to modern contemporary society. At the same time, those who were fond of the medieval era or felt nostalgia for imperial Spain received the criticism of unofficial historiography, which ultimately transmitted an image of a history of Spain little different from that of Europe.[21] Comparison with what was considered characteristic of the recent history of the democratic countries of the West did, however, reveal one feature specific to the development of Spain: the lack of dynamism in everything connected with social change. There had been no revolution of an intensity similar to that of the one that took place in France or other parts of Europe but instead a change of a political nature in a timidly liberal direction. The ultimate reason, it was thought then, was the country's economic backwardness and the absence of a middle class that was a natural consequence of that backwardness. By contrast with the more advanced countries of Europe, which experienced industrialization and the rise of an enterprising middle class, the Spain of the nineteenth century was characterized by the dominion of the old nobility and by a society and a dual economy in which sector and class features of an incomplete transition coexisted. The economic, political, and ideological weakness of the middle classes contrasted with the prestige and social power of blue-blooded aristocrats, large landowners, and leaders in the area of finance. The oligarchical power bloc that was created in the nineteenth century, after a liberal revolution that had left intact the economic foundations of the power of the old aristocracy, had thus proved to be a hindrance to economic development and evolution towards democracy.

Onto this image, which had many points in common with liberal historiography prior to the victory of Franco's dictatorship, two kinds of influences were superimposed in the 1970s during the transition from dictatorship to democracy – influences that in the end modified it without going so far as to question it. The first was explicitly Marxist in orientation, but it would be false to attribute to it the economicism and dogmatism of the political ideology that inspired it. Although there was and still is that kind of Marxism in Spanish historiography, one of the few debates to have attained a certain importance in Spain – whether there had been a 'middle-class revolution' during the nineteenth century – revealed not one but several ways of conceiving Marxism to explain the history of Spain, some of which were so 'heterodox' that they anticipated conclusions about the revolutionary process later judged to be 'revisionist' in the rest of Europe. The second influence, evident since the 1970s, came from the 'new economic history' and the 'new political history' that began to develop as an alternative to the influence of Marxism. Both initially put the accent on the obstacles to modernization in the course of the nineteenth and twentieth centuries.

POLITICS AND HISTORY IN THE 1990s

Gradually, what had been a view of history dominated by the idea of Spain's economic and political backwardness acquired a completely different significance. During most of the twentieth century the awareness of this backwardness by comparison with the development of the other democratic states of Western Europe had led to an emphasis on two disasters, the loss of the last remains of the American empire in 1898 and the Civil War of 1936–39, which brought out the magnitude of the catastrophe and 'Spain's failure'. For a long time these two events created a sense of shock in the historical and political consciousness of Spaniards. If only because of the lack of a democratic regime, the political situation in the final period of the dictatorship and the beginning of the negotiated transition seemed to justify the hypercritical attitude of historians towards our past. Once democracy began to consolidate, however, a different image of the history of Spain began to win supporters. This image increasingly emphasized its similarity to the path followed by the more advanced countries in Europe and played down the importance of the 'failures' mentioned. In the past decade a good many historians have gradually begun to question the classic theses of progressive historiography (liberal-nationalist, either economic and social or Marxist-influenced) and instead to stress the image of a 'normal' historical development that could not be perceived until now, either inside or outside the country, for fundamentally ideological reasons.[22]

The fact that the commemorations enthusiastically supported by the governments of one political tendency or another have openly profited from this new paradigm which insists on the normality of our history should nevertheless have put the revisionist historians – so critical of the ideologies of the past – on their guard. The first of the commemorations that clearly drew political advantage from the results of the current revisionism was the one that took place in 1988, on the occasion of the bicentenary of the death of Charles III. Both the monarchy and the enlightened ministers who governed in that period with the monarchy's consent were presented as agents of the modernization of the country considerably before the outbreak of the French Revolution. They thus became an encouraging antecedent for the current democratic monarchy of King Juan Carlos I and the third course followed by the Socialist government, showing its equidistance from the old revolutionary aspirations of the classical left and the extreme conservatism of the right that has almost always governed Spain. As a timely complement, in 1992 the quincentenary of the 'discovery' of America brought, in the words of the historian José María Jover, 'a kind of veneer of universality enhancing the recent glad tidings that henceforth we were to be Europeans and that the years of isolation after the Civil War were gone for good'.[23] Very shortly before, the Socialist government – an enthusiastic promoter of both commemorations – had succeeded in making Spain a full member of North Atlantic Treaty Organization, going against what had previously been the political posture of the party that sustained it.

In the final years of the Socialist period, however, there was a surprising change. Suddenly a mood of crisis and mistrust set in, with a great wave of accusations of corruption involving people close to Felipe González's government. This mood placed a question mark over the optimistic image of Spain's historical normality, and there was a revival of the old doom-laden view of a corrupt Spain in which, under the cloak of politics, *caciques* and clienteles proliferated. The economic and financial scandals and the discovery of the political conspiracy of the GAL (Grupos Antiterroristas de Liberación) (an antiterrorist group that had exercised violence against the circles of the Basque separatist ETA with the complicity even of certain officials of the Ministry of the Interior) indicated the inheritance of a system that had survived from the dictatorship as a result of concessions to the past made during the transition.

In this context, in 1994 the best-selling history book *Breve historia de España,* by Fernando García de Cortázar and José Manuel González Vesga, put forward the idea of an 'unfinished Spain', constantly passing through areas of light and shade along its path. After experiencing an exemplary transition to democracy during the governments of Adolfo Suárez and the first Socialist era, Spain was by then in full recession, with a government that was exercising a monopoly of control of public institutions or acting as a 'front for the phenomena of corruption that mark the end of the third Socialist legislature', 'an industry dismantled by competition from European products, a disoriented agriculture and the unstoppable growth of unemployment', 'a materialistic society devoid of utopias' and 'the radicalization of the *nationalist* movements'.[24]

This panorama, which suddenly had become so contrary to the exaggerated optimism of a few years earlier, was described in such apocalyptic tones that it was possible to see through it to the political purpose of the accusation. In addition to the discrediting of Felipe González, who had headed the government for too long and was by then suspected of seeking to perpetuate himself at the cost of Spain's interests, democracy was identified with an alternation of power in favour of a party – the Popular Party – that came from the traditional right and needed to occupy the political centre, until then in the hands of the Socialists, in order to win the election. While the Socialists remained immersed in impotence, incapable of cleansing their image by means of a self-criticism that might restore their credibility and bring about the replacement of their leaders, the Popular Party put together a skilful strategy that brought it to power in 1996.

After the change of government, with the same speed as before but this time in the opposite direction, the doom-laden tones were suspiciously replaced by a view that revived the encouraging normality of a historical course about to culminate in Spain's full integration into the new united Europe. The use of historiographic revisionism has been evident in the anniversaries enthusiastically supported by the Popular Party government.

Thus the 'disaster' of a century ago (the 'crisis of 1898') ended up being presented as an exaggeration on the part of intellectuals steeped in radicalism and demagoguery, unable to understand the extent to which, thanks to the efforts of the Liberal politicians of the time, Spain was then following the course of economic modernization and politics pursued by countries of the Western world.[25] Far from being a historical rarity in our country, liberalism had a long tradition of modest successes back at least as far as the Restoration years under Cánovas. At the same time, Cánovas was rehabilitated as a true statesman who had been attacked by extremists of both tendencies. His regime, contrary to progressive or Marxist historiography, was declared to have had very positive effects. It had been able to put a stop to militarism for a long period, establish a system for the enjoyment of rights and freedoms equivalent to those of the most advanced countries in Europe, and create a climate of social peace that made possible the development of the Spanish economy. In the context of this kind of historiographic revisionism, highly favourable to the achievements of the Restoration regime but as exaggeratedly partial as the earlier scathing criticism, it is not surprising that the Popular Party took advantage of Cánovas's centenary to convert him into the great precursor of their policies.[26] It had been much harder for the Conservative leader Manuel Fraga Iribarne when he championed Cánovas, at a time when revisionist history did not yet exist and the predominant view was of a backward Spain in the hands of oligarchs and *caciques*.

Finally, the pretext of the quarter-centenary of the death of Philip II offered a further opportunity to use history for political ends, with a Spanish nationalist smugness that succeeded in wounding the sensibilities of Portuguese neighbours at Expo 98 in Lisbon. The supposed universality of which Jover spoke to us in connection with the quincentenary of the 'discovery' of America was now reinforced by a staging interested only in highlighting the splendour of a reign full of brilliance in the spheres of art and culture.[27] Seen in this light, Philip II was a prince of the Renaissance willing to govern a great 'confederation of territories' with wisdom and humanity – a king, according to the historian Henry Kamen, who pursued 'universal pleasures and interests' although 'imbued with a deep religiosity like most rulers of the time'.[28] The book by this scholar of Spanish affairs, *Philip of Spain*, has also been a best-seller,[29] and, as Antonio Elorza rightly foresaw, it set the pattern for 'the commemorative image of the great king who inspired the name of the current heir to the Spanish throne'.[30] This desire on the part of our current rulers to display the most brilliant, normalized, acceptable part of our past – art, science, universalism – from a European perspective, setting aside social manifestations that have become less presentable and the conflicts that formerly marked us, now appears with very suspicious self-satisfied reiteration. This happened once again in connection with the crisis of 1898[31] and has been repeated in exhibitions such as the one recently organized by the Valencian Autonomous Government and the Archbishopric of Valencia on 'the important part played by the Church in the historical development of the Valencian Community and the wealth of an artistic and cultural legacy that is to a large extent unknown'.[32] The title of the exhibition, 'The Light of Images', is highly illustrative; the darker areas, evidently, do not deserve to be remembered.

The current historiographic revisionism also has other political uses that are more worrying because of the intention that they reveal. Until very recently – in due correspondence with the optimism promoted by the current conjuncture of democratic stability and economic success, which, as we have seen, has modified our image of the past and lifted it out of its obsession with backwardness and decline – a veil of oblivion and caution had been drawn over our more recent history. Timely reference to this is made in Paloma Aguilar Fernández's book *Memoria y olvido de la guerra civil española*,[33] and this situation, which, as we have seen, at the time worked in favour of the reconciliation of Spaniards, could now have effects that might run counter to the establishment of democratic values. The demythologizing of the Republican side that is beginning to appear in historical research is clearly not the problem. Part of the work of historians constantly to revise what has been written about the past and to highlight any kind of ideological influence on the different ways of studying a historical event. The problem is the one-sided, tendentious way in which the results of this research are being presented to a broad public and the unusual interest aroused by these studies, especially when they are concerned with combating the image of those who fought on the Republican side during the 1936–39 war (this is the case with the International Brigades, to give one example) or covertly seeking a partial rehabilitation of Franco's regime and of his person – in the final analysis, a pioneer in the victorious struggle against revolutionary socialism, as subsequently one of his admirers in Chile, General Augusto Pinochet, would also appear to have been. The defeat of communism and the success of modernization in our country thus seem to be connected with a 'really not very fascist' regime, supposedly with an authoritarian ideology that was not particularly firm and consequently was capable of admitting internal dissidence which later made possible the pact leading to democracy. Such a falsification of history, as some historians have recently charged, overlooks the degree to which Franco's dictatorship was radically antiliberal, the extent to which it repressed democrats of all kinds, and the way in which, until the very end, it hung on to its desire to be perpetuated, something that proved impossible as Spanish society developed and became integrated into Europe.

Finally, in contrast to the situation during the years of struggle against the dictatorship, the idea of highlighting the diverse, plural reality of our country and at the same time pointing to its a common history seems to have little support. Works of synthesis offering a history of the 'autonomous communities' provoke an angry reaction from advocates of a single history of the 'Spanish nation', who see the former approach as propitiating nationalist separatisms or becoming locked in localism. The debate has extended into the area of the education of children and adolescents and the question of what kinds of history should be taught nowadays.[34] Criticizing and demythologizing any kind of use of history for nationalist ends does not seem to have been defended consistently by a good many of the participants in this debate. This, at least, is the situation when the very individuals who present timely, well grounded criticism of Spanish historiographic nationalism nevertheless defend a nationalist history in the case of Catalonia (or the Catalan Lands), Euskal Herria, or Galicia. And the same could be said of those who are in favour of dismantling myths about origins and nationalist manipulations of history when it is a question of these other nationalisms but who are none too willing to detach themselves from the idea of a Spanish national development basically identified with the history of the predominance of one society, one language and one culture (Castile). Three examples may serve to illustrate this: the controversy in Catalonia about the development of its historiography,[35] the recent debate about the teaching of the humanities already mentioned (and the conception of the current Ministry of Culture and Education, the historians who have advised it, and the intellectuals who have applauded it, not exactly of right-wing origin), and the recent award of a national essay prize to the collective book *El ser de España*.[36] No doubt we should connect all this with the current debate about whether there is a need to reform the democratic Constitution of 1978 in the context of the demands for a greater degree of self-government put forward by peripheral nationalisms.

As stated at the outset, history has an important political part to play in the current situation. The special feature of Spain among the Mediterranean countries in connection with the political uses of the past is apparent, broadly speaking, in a development bounded by two *fin-de-siècle* crises of very different kinds. A hundred years ago, the disaster represented by the loss of the last remnants of the colonial empire was evident to all. From that crisis a kind of 'regenerationist' nationalism emerged that advocated replacing the old state of notables or oligarchs characteristic of a backward agrarian society with a different, more modern one supported by new social groups. The current crisis, however, must be set in a totally different social and political context. Its cause is not industrialization or any colonial disaster or general sense of backwardness in relation to other countries. The statement 'Spain is doing well', made by the Prime Minister, José María Aznar, immediately after coming to power in 1996, reveals the inordinate optimism that invades the country now, contrasting with the equally exaggerated pessimism of a century ago. If there is a crisis in Spain today it is certainly for other reasons, especially the awareness that the globalization to which Spain is tending is numbering the days of the nation-state just as it is in other parts of Europe.

In another context, therefore, very different from that of a century ago, in Spain too the various groups that dispute hegemony have linked their respective political projects to conflicting views of the past. At first sight it would seem that we are faced with a new edition of the old, interminable debate about the 'problem of Spain',[37] first put forward during the crisis at the end of the nineteenth century. However, the area of the debate is utterly different. Whereas 100 years ago the 'problem of Spain' arose from an awareness that its history was one that included numerous failures and an extraordinary decline, now the immediate future of a united Europe, in which for some years Spain has been playing a leading role, is tending to erase differences and highlight similarities in a development in which only successes are of interest. In this new European context, those who consider Spain's existence as a nation unchallengeable are advocates of a history that reinforces the collective feeling of belonging to that 'incontrovertible reality'. For those who think that Spain as a collective entity must gradually give way to other identities, in contrast, recourse to history serves to legitimize other political options that may favour the maximum autonomy or even independence of hitherto stateless nations in the not too distant future.

However, anyone who thinks that the current debate will in future take place on the same intellectual horizon as in the past is mistaken. Although a revival of conflict between nationalist ideologies appealing to history remains very likely, the fact is that in the new era that we are entering the crisis of national identities classically conceived – with or without a state – is becoming increasingly apparent. Internal cultural homogenization and the exclusion of those who do not share the features of an identity that, after all, can always be reinvented are becoming increasingly meaningless. Our world is tending towards multiculturalism, and the coexistence and superimposition of multifarious identities capable of resolving conflicts by means of dialogue and communication make it necessary to think about a new political use of history. This new use will be sorely needed to provide an impulse for the future development of societies that will increasingly be experiencing both globalization and internal differentiation. If historians take refuge in scientific asepsis at this crucial moment, others will go on using history to legitimize old powers and impose identities that will perpetuate the current conflicts.

Translated by Karel Clapshaw

NOTES

1. See, for example, some of the more important controversies included in H.-U. Wehler, *Politik in der Geschichte* (Munich, 1998).
2. Referring only to recent publications, see *Afers*, 25 (1996); *Ayer*, 33 (1999); and the review of some of the more outstanding books and articles in S. Juliá, 'Un fascismo bajo Palio, en uniforme militar', *Babelia-El País*, 349 (18 July 1998). Reference to the polemic unleashed in Italy by the attempt by S. Romano and I. Montanelli to revise the figure of Franco and his political regime is made by M.A. Macciocchi in 'Franco y los revisionistas', *El País* (26 June 1998).
3. *Ayer*, 15 (1994); J. Tusell and Á. Soto (eds.), *Historia de la transición 1975–1986* (Madrid, 1996).
4. See the polemic aroused by the article by J. Marías, 'El artículo más iluso', *El País* (26 June 1999).
5. In barely two months at the end of 1997, according to the data of the Ministry of Education, 650 essays and editorials appeared in the Spanish press.
6. I. Peiró, *Los guardianes de la historia* (Saragossa, 1995).
7. Pierre Nora (ed.), *Les lieux de mémoire*, 3 Vols. (Paris, 1997). For its reception in Spain, see *Ayer*, 32 (1998).
8. See the references in J. Cuesta, 'Memoria e historia: Un estado de la cuestión', *Ayer*, 23 (1998), pp.203–46.
9. F. García de Cortázar and J.M. González Vesga, *Breve historia de España* (Madrid, 1994); J. Tusell (ed.), *Historia de España* (Madrid, 1998).
10. Reference is made to this in the contributions to *Ayer*, 30 (1998).
11. Jeffrey Olick, 'Memoria colectiva y diferenciación cronológica: Historicidad y ámbito público', *Ayer*, 32 (1998), pp.119–45.
12. In fact, going beyond metaphors, Spanish nationalist music is late and exceptional (Falla, Albéniz).
13. For this further problem, see the controversy between B. de Riquer and J.P. Fusi in *Historia Social*, 7 (1990), pp.105–35; the article by B. de Riquer, 'Naciones y regiones: Problemas en torno a la débil nacionalización del siglo XIX', included in the collection edited A. Morales Moya and M.E. de Vega, *La historia contemporánea de España* (Salamanca, 1996), pp.73–89; J. Álvarez Junco, 'La nación en duda', in J. Pan-Motojo (ed.), *Más se perdió en Cuba: España, 1898 y la crisis fin de siglo* (Madrid, 1998), pp.405–75; J.M. Fradera, *Cultura nacional en una societat divida: Patriotisme i cultura a Catalunya (1836–1868)* (Barcelona, 1992).
14. I emphasize the aspect of *process* to call attention to what has been written about the modern conception of history by H. Arendt in 'Historia e inmortalidad', included in *De la historia a la acción* (Barcelona, 1995), pp.47–73, and R. Koselleck, *Futuro pasado: Para una semántica de los tiempos históricos* (Barcelona, 1993).
15. Some of the primary school textbooks that were extensively used in the 1920s are a good indication of this: the *Compendio de historia de España* by G.M. Bruño, the *Compendio de historia de España* by the Piarist priest Francisco Asensi, and others.
16. The supporting texts are from the 1940s and 1950s, focusing on the teaching of history; see the analysis by R. Valls in *La interpretacion de la historia de Espana y sus origenes ideológicos en el bachillerato franquista (1938–1953)* (Valencia, 1984), and E. Martínez Tórtola, *La enseñanza de la historia en el primer bachillerato franquista* (Madrid, 1996). One of the first attempts at historical legitimation of the figure of Franco and his regime is *Laureados de España*, published in the 'Year of Victory' (Madrid, 1939), with contributions by, among many others, J. Penmartín, Fr. J. Pérez de Urbel, M. Machado, G. Diego, C.J. Cela, V. de la Serna, and J.I. Luca de Tena. On the historiography of the early Franco period, see the interesting work by G. Pasamar, *Historiografía en la postguerra española: La ruptura de la tradición liberal* (Saragossa, 1991).

17. See, for example, the long list of historical novels and 'national episodes' by B. Pérez Galdós. For the Marquis of Lozoya, in *La concepción romántica de la historia* (Valencia, 1930), the key to the success of liberal ideology in the late nineteenth century was the cultivation of history and historical novels of higher literary quality than those of the traditionalists.
18. See especially the chapter devoted to him by C.P. Boyd in *Historia Patria: Politics, History, and National Identity in Spain, 1875–1975* (Princeton, 1997), highly recommended, incidentally, on the subject that we are considering.
19. The most obvious case is the book, later made into a play, by A. Sopeña Monsalve, *El florido pensil: Memoria de la escuela nacionalcatólica* (Barcelona, 1994).
20. The development of Spanish historiography during the 1950s, 1960s and early 1970s can be seen in the overall appraisal made in 1974 by J.M. Jover, recently republished with the title 'El siglo XIX en la historiografía española de la época de Franco' in his *Historiadores españoles de nuestro siglo* (Madrid, 1999).
21. Reference must be made to the Catalan historian Jaume Vicens Vives, one of the most outstanding figures in the historiographical renovation in Spain. See the book by J.M. Muñoz Lloret, *Jaume Vicens i Vives: Una biografia intellectual* (Barcelona, 1997).
22. Exponents of this are the numerous works mentioned by S. Juliá in his article 'Anomalía, dolor y fracaso de España', *Claves de Razón Práctica*, 66 (1996), pp.10–21. Comparison with an earlier article of his, 'Transiciones a la democracia', *Sistema*, 84 (1988), pp.25–40, shows the change that has taken place in him in the past ten years. Juliá is, however, one of the historians who have fought most resolutely in the media against viewing Spain as a country with a normal historical development without taking into account other much less comparable aspects of our past. The book by J.P. Fusi and J. Palafox, *España 1808–1896: El desafío de la modernidad* (Madrid, 1997), one of the best-sellers of recent years, is possibly the work most representative of the revisionism that radically questions the exceptional nature of Spain and abandons the 'myth of failure'. See C. Powell's interview with J.P. Fusi at the time of the book's publication in the literary supplement of the newspaper *ABC* (28 Nov. 1997).
23. J.M. Jover, 'El centenario que viene', *El País* (10 Dec. 1996), p.13
24. García de Cortázar and González Vesga, *Breve historia de España*, Ch.1, pp.53–7.
25. This is the interpretation offered by J.M. Marco in *La libertad traicionada* (Barcelona, 1997), a book that made a particular impact on the public after being presented by the prime minister, José María Aznar.
26. An option that can be understood only if one views the Cánovas period as favourably as does recent historiography but proves curious and significant in the light of the timely comment made by A. Elorza in 'Una pasión excesiva', *El País* (24 Aug. 1997): 'However much the pill is sugared, the place of Cánovas in history is closer to authoritarian conservatism than modernizing liberalism'. In the same context of criticism of the recovery of Cánovas by the Spanish right, see the article by S. Juliá, 'Gran estadista, ruina de Estado', *El País* (20 Aug. 1997).
27. See the splendid catalogue for the exhibition *Felipe II, un monarca y su época: Un príncipe del renacimiento*, presented at the Museo Nacional del Prado in Madrid from 13 Oct. 1998 to 10 Jan. 1999.
28. Quoted literally by the journalist M.Á. Villena in *El País* (5 Nov. 1998) in a debate that elicited considerable response in the media, with the participation of Geoffrey Parker, author of *The Grand Strategy of Philip II* (New Haven, 1998). For Parker, an authoritarian nature and religious fundamentalism are two notable characteristics of the Spanish monarch's personality, which is a long way, therefore, from the positive view that has predominated in the official commemorative acts.
29. Published in Spanish as *Felipe de España* (Madrid, 1997), it reached a third impression between May and August of that year, something quite extraordinary for that kind of book in Spain.

30. A. Elorza, 'Crisis del imperio', *El País* (17 Jan. 1998).
31. The exhibition 'España fin de siglo 1898', which opened at the former Museo Español de Arte Contemporáneo on 9 Jan. 1998, presenting a mixture of 'erudition and beauty', as reported in the account that appeared in the newspapers, and delving into the other side of 1898: not the colonial disaster and the accusations made by the writers of the generation of '98 but the daily reality and everyday life, the economic and cultural continuity despite the loss of the colonies, and the scientific advances and improvements in health. The exhibition 'Un siglo de ciencia en España', which opened at the Residencia de Estudiantes on 23 Dec. 1998, concluded the events that reviewed the centenary of 1898.
32. Quoted from the guide to the exhibition 'La luz de las imágenes', published by the Generalitat Valenciana. The exhibition was a considerable public success, so much so that the organizers were obliged to extend it.
33. P. Aguilar, *Memoria y olvido de la guerra civil española (1936–1939)* (Madrid, 1996).
34. I have referred to this in 'La historia en el debate político sobre la enseñanza de las humanidades', *Ayer*, 30 (1998), pp.63–100.
35. Partially included in the book by A. Balcells, *La història de Catalunya a debat: Els textos d'una polèmica* (Barcelona, 1994).
36. Real Academia de la Historia, *España: Reflexiones sobre el ser de España* (Madrid, 1997). An intelligent critique of the political background was made by J.S. Pérez Garzón, 'Españoleando con la historia de la Academia', in *El País*, 9 Dec. 1998.
37. See J. Varela, *La novela de España: Los intelectuales y el problema español* (Madrid, 1999).

Abstracts

Towards an Ethnographic Phenomenology of the Greek Spirit, *by Michael Herzfeld*

This article is an attempt to question the literalistic interpretation of nationalist ideologies, especially that of Greece, as accurate representations of either the cultural and social experiences of citizens or the practical experiences of administrators. The force of such ideologies in Greece owes a great deal to the historical and political specificities of the country's domination by powers determined to use it as a frontier of European civilization and supported by local elites in that endeavour. Concealment – in a range of cultural activities from religion to architecture – permits the expression of alternative notions of identity, entailing the recognition of very different histories; historic conservation is an especially interesting battleground for such contestation of the official past. A comparison of Greece with Italy highlights contrasting dynamics in the production of local and national histories.

The Construction of National Time: The Making of the Modern Greek Historical Imagination, *by Antonis Liakos*

The national narrative restructures the experience of time, presenting the nation as an active historical agent that, through the narrative, acquires a new historical identity. The Mediterranean nations have undertaken the difficult task of combining different significant pasts. The appropriation and resignification of these pasts involve adjustment of different perceptions of the structure of time. This article explores the making of modern Greek national history through this process.

Shifting Boundaries, Clientalism and Balkan Identities, *by Drago Roksandič*

Comparative historical research in the Mediterranean area is difficult. Mediterranean Europe, Mediterranean Asia, and Mediterranean Africa are the uneven relevance in the frameworks of their respective continents, and each point on the Mediterranean shore has a tradition of contacts of different kinds with the quasi-totality of the Mediterranean world. The tradition of nation-states in the Mediterranean area, though often deeply rooted, are a modern phenomenon. Each of them involves a controversial appropriation of a desired heritage that could usually be appropriated by someone else. In the Balkans, which have since antiquity been the meeting place of various competing imperial interests, the conviction is widespread that a nation must assert its right to protection in terms of the exceptional aspects of its identity in opposition to those of its neighbours. The experience on these countries has facilitated the emergence of national myths prepared to justify intolerance towards the 'other' and even legitimize it in terms of some universal value. The fragility of these national myths leaves little room for the application of comparative approaches across national borders.

Notes on Two Discordant Histories: Armenia during World War I, ***by Lucette Valensi***

The article deals with historiographic issues of the Armenian question. The debate taking place between different narratives of Armenian and Turkish historians places at its centre the political uses of history. The purpose of this article is to lay the groundwork for the Armenian–Turkish debate, to articulate the terms of the discourse, and to try to understand the confrontation between the parties through an examination of a varied spectrum of historical narratives and attitudes.

The Distant Past: On the Political Use of History, ***by Giovanni Levi***

Through the examination of examples of the recent political use of history, it is argued here that the relationship between historiography and its readers has changed dramatically. With the proliferation of new mass media, the book has lost its centrality. As a consequence, simplified information rapidly produced is replacing the complex picture that the discipline has traditionally assembled. Memory has also changed: individual memory has replaced the social and collective memory on which historical work has been built. With the end of bipolarism and the collapse of the Soviet system has come a new historical revisionism that, instead of reassessing the political and ideological ideas of the past, proposes a generalized depreciation of it. Because the past is considered to have been entirely negative, we cannot look to history for values to guide the future. The political use of the past by the Catholic Church has played a powerful role in strengthening this negative image.

The Two Levels of Public Use of the Past, ***by Claudio Pavone***

The public use of history is as ancient as history itself. It exists on two levels, one scientific and academic and the other performing the everyday function of helping to create common historical knowledge. Both uses are legitimate and constantly refer to each other, but one must be careful not to confuse the two. Public use is also made of both individual and group memory, which is woven into history. Modern nation-states have made wide use of history as an instrument of nation building. In Italy, a country unified only in 1861 but with ancient cultural traditions, the past has been much used, often in contradictory ways, by the liberal regime, by Fascism, and then by the democratic republic. Fascism tried, with little success, to transform the history of ancient Rome into popular myth. Today discussion centres on the Italian Risorgimento, Fascism and anti-Fascism, World War II, the Resistance, and the advent of the republic created in 1946.

Out of Place, Out of Time, ***by Elias Sanbar***

The article presents the case of the Palestinians as a prism through which the question of political uses of history can be addressed. The claim is that 1948, the year of the *Nakba*, a key date in the history of the Palestinian people, was a rupture in the continuity of historical space and time in Palestinian history. The article discusses the formation of the Palestinian national identity, both in relation to the *Nakba*, and to the Palestinian exile and demonstrates the intense and formative relationship between the *Nakba* and formation of Palestinian national identity. History, to the extent that served as a buffer to guard against disappearance, became an 'emergency science' among Palestinians. The article draws attention to certain historical approaches that have evolved in the last decades, and points to key genres of historiography, and their relation to the notion of 'disappearance from history' of the Palestinian people.

Political Uses of History in Spain, ***by Pedro Ruiz Torres***

History has always been a target of political exploitation. Two opposed conception of Spanish history confronted one another throughout most of the twentieth century. With no tradition of memory/history or hegemonic national consciousness, the years of dictatorship accentuated the old conflict. The way in which the transition to democracy took place encouraged the forgetting of our most recent past. We are now witnessing an increasing politicization of history in a way less evident than before. Historical commemorations and revisions present an interested picture of normality that contrasts with the pessimism of yesteryear.

List of Contributors

François Hartog is directeur d'études at the École des Hautes Etudes en Sciences Sociales in Paris. His works deal with ancient and modern historiography. His recent publications include *L'Histoire d'Homère à Augustin* (Paris, 1999); *Le miroir d'Hérodote* (Paris, 2001); *Le XIXe siècle et l'histoire: le cas Fustel de Coulanges* (Paris, 2001).

Michael Herzfeld is Professor of Anthropology at Harvard University and a past editor of the *American Ethnologist*. His research in Greece has generated, in addition to the works cited in this article, *The Poetics of Manhood: Contest and Identity in a Cretan Mountain Village* (Princeton, 1985) and *Portrait of a Greek Imagination: An Ethnographic Biography of Andreas Nenedakis* (Chicago, 1997). Currently engaged in research on the politics of the past in Rome, he is also planning research on related topics in Thailand.

Giovanni Levi is Professor of Early Modern History at Ca' Foscari University in Venice. He was editor (with C. Ginzburg) of the Microstoria series, one of the volumes of which is his *Eredità Immateriale* (1985), since translated into nine languages. His main books are *Centro e Periferia di uno Stato Assoluto* (Turin, 1985), *History of Youth* (edited with J.C. Schmitt, Paris, 1994, *Microhistoria* (Buenos Aires, 1996), and *Ejercicios de historia social* (Valencia, 2001). He is currently working on consumption in early modern Italy.

Antonis Liakos is Professor of Contemporary History at the University of Athens. He is the author of *Labour and Politics in Interwar Greece* (Athens, 1993), and *L'Unificazione italiana e la Grande idea* (Florence, 1995). His main research areas are the nineteenth century in Greece and Italy, social history, and the history of historiography.

Claudio Pavone took part in the Italian Resistance. He worked in the Italian State Archives from 1950 to 1974, and taught contemporary history at the University of Pisa from 1975 to 1991. His studies deal mostly with the history of institutions, the administration of the Italian state, the Fascist period, World War II, and the Resistance. He is the author of *Una Guerra Civile: Saggio Storico sulla Moralità nella Resistenza* (Turin, 1991), and a co-editor of *Guida Generale degli Archivi di Stato italiani* (Rome, 1981).

Jacques Revel has been the president of l'École des Hautes Études en Sciences Sociales since 1995. A graduate of l'École Normale Supérieure (Ulm), where he majored in History, he is a member of l'École française de Rome, and specializes in the sociocultural history of Modern Europe, with particular interest in historiographical issues. Among his publications are *Une politique de la langue* (en coll., 1975), *Les Universités européennes à l'époque moderne* (en coll., 1986–89), *Logiques de la foule* (en coll., 1988), *Histoire de la France* (en coll., 4 vols., 1989–93), *Jeux d'échelles* (1996), *Histories. French Constructions of the Past* (en coll., 1996).

Drago Roksandič is head of the History Department at the University of Zagreb and a member of the History Department of the CEU in Budapest, Hungary. His major works include *Military Croatia* (Zagreb, 1988), *The Serbian and Croatian Past and the 'New History'* (Zagreb, 1991), *Serbs in Croatia* (Zagreb, 1991), *Against the War* (Zagreb, 1996), and (with Natasa Stefanec) the edited collection *Constructing the Border Societies on the Triplex Confinium* (Budapest, 2000).

Pedro Ruiz Torres is University Professor of Contemporary History and Rector of the University of Valencia. He is the author or co-author of *Estudios sobre la revolución burguesa en España* (Madrid, 1979), *España en el siglo XVIII (Homenaje a Pierre Vilar)* (Barcelona, 1985); *La época de la razón* (Barcelona, 1993), *Reformas y políticas agrarias en la historia de España* (Madrid, 1996), and *Discursos sobre la historia* (Valencia, 2000).

Elias Sanbar is the editor of the *Revue d'études palestiniennes*. He was the leader of the Palestinian delegation to the multilateral negotiations for peace on the subject of Palestinian refugees between 1993 and 1996. Among his recent publication is a translation of *La Terre nous est etroite et autres poèmes (1966–1999)* (Paris, 2000).

Lucette Valensi is a historian of North Africa and the Middle East. Among her books in English are *On the Eve of Colonialism: North Africa Before the French Conquest* (New York, 1977), *Tunisian Peasants in the 18th and 19th Century* (Cambridge, 1985), (with N. Wachtel) *Jewish Memories* (Berkeley, 1991), and *The Birth of the Despot: Venice and the Sublime Porte* (Ithaca, NY, 1993). Her latest book in French is *Fables de la mémoire: La glorieuse bataille des Trois Rois* (Paris, 1992).

Index

Acre, 89
Adriatic Sea, 82
Africa, 43, 71, 81, 82
  East Africa, 81
  North Africa, 2
Ahmad, Feroz, 54
Aix-en-Provence, 81
Albania, 45, 47
Aleppo, 51
Alexander the Great, 16, 19
Algeria, 49, 82
Algerian War, 2
Allende, Salvador, 97
Alps, 77–8
Altamira, Rafael, 104
America, 95, 96, 101, 102, 108, *see also* United States
American Revolution, 2, 69
American University of Beirut, 92
Anatolia, *see* Asia Minor
Anderson, Benedict, 28
'Arif, 'Arif al-, 92
Armenia, Armenians, 4, 9, 49–58, 71
Asia, 43
Asia Minor, 14, 38, 49, 52
Atatürk, 33, 57
Athens, 16, 23, 24, 35
  University of Athens, 34, 39
Aubrac, Lucie, 10, 11n, 12n
Aubrac, Raymond, 10, 11n, 12n
Auschwitz, 70
Austria, 69, 77
Aymard, Maurice, 82
Aznar, José María, 113, 115n

Balkans, 4, 14, 25n, 29, 38, 45–7, 66, 71, 81, 82
Balmes, Jaime, 103
Barbie, Klaus, 12n
Barth, Frederik, 27
Battini, M., 81
Bavaria, 21
Berlusconi, Silvio, 64
Bertoldi, Silvio, 84
Bion, W.R., 66
Bir al-Sab', 89
Bloch, Marc, 6, 75
Blondel, M., 78
Bolland, Jean, 78
Bonfante, Giuliano, 62, 63
Bousquet, 5
Braude, Benjamin, 54
Braudel, Fernand, 43
Bulgaria, 29, 45
Byron, Lord George, 32
Byzantium, 29, 32, 33, 34, 35, 42n

Caesar, 2
Caluire, 11n
Cambodia, 71
Campidoglio, 79
Cánovas del Castillo, Antonio, 96, 110, 115n
Casini, Carlo, 64
Castile, 104
Casucci, Costanzo, 81
Catalonia, 64, 96, 112
Ceausescu, Nicolae, 63
Cenci, Cristina, 79
Charles III, King, 96, 104, 108
Charles IV, King, 104
Charles V, King, 102
Chicago, 22
Chile, 97, 111
China, 71
Cilicia, 51
Clifford, James, 62
Coleman, Janet, 67
Constantinople, *see* Istanbul
Contini, G., 81
Copeaux, Etienne, 54
Corfu, 17
Corsica, 81
Corttés, Donoso, 103
Covadonga, 102
Croatia, 45, 70
Croce, Benedetto, 76

Dalmatia, 81, 82
De Felice, Renzo, 74
Del Boca, A., 83
Dimaras, Constantine, 38, 40
Dimitrov, Georgi, 63
Dionisotti, Carlo, 79
Djemal, Pasha, 51
Dreyfus affair, 1
Droysen, Johann Gustav, 32, 35
Dumont, Paul, 55

Egypt, 29, 82, 88, 89
El Cide, 102
Elitis, Odisseas, 39
English Civil War, 69

Enver, Pasha, 51
Ethiopia, 84
Euphrates, 88
Europe, 35, 36, 43, 46, 47, 64, 67, 77, 81, 87, 95, 101, 103, 105, 107, 111, 113
Eastern Europe, 14
Western Europe, 34, 38, 108
European Parliament, 56
European Union, 23, 24
Euskal Herria, 112

Farouqui, Sulayman al-Taji al-, 90
Fauriel, Claude, 18
Febvre, Lucien, 77
Ferdinand VII, King, 105
Fernández, Paloma Aguilar, 111
Fiesole, 85
Final Solution, 71
Forti, C., 81
Fortunato, Giustino, 81
France, 2, 3, 5, 9, 10, 43, 65, 77, 82, 83, 98–9, 103, 107
Franco, Francisco, 62–3, 78, 96, 97, 101, 102, 104, 105, 111
French Revolution, 2, 3, 69, 96, 108
Freud, Sigmund, 54, 58n
Fueter, E., 78
Furet, François, 61

Galicia, 112
Galilee, 89
Galileo Galilei, 83
Gallerano, Nicola, 74
Galli della Loggia, Ernesto, 84
García de Cortázar, Fernando, 100, 109
Garzón, Baltasar, 97
Gaza, 89
Gellner, Ernest, 28
Georgeon, François, 55
Germany, 5, 25, 51, 66, 95, 103
Gheorghiu-Dej, Gheorghe, 63
Gibbon, Edward, 32
Ginzburg, Carlo, 11, 76
Gioberti, Abbot Vincenzo, 79
González, Felipe, 109
Gottwald, Klement, 63
Great Britain, 82, 87
History Workshops movement, 5
Greece, 3, 13–25, 29, 30, 31, 33, 35, 36, 37, 38, 42n, 45, 78
Grotowohl, Otto, 63
Guilford, Lord, 16

Habermas, Jürgen, 4, 8, 74
Haifa, 89
Hatzidakis, Manos, 39
Hatzimihali, Angeliki, 39
Hayden, Robert, 14
Hebron, 89
Hegel, Friedrich, 32
Herzfeld, Michael, 3
Hobsbawm, Eric, 28, 84
Holocaust, 70
Hourani, Faysal, 94
Hovannisian, Richard, 52

Ionian Sea, 82
Iribarne, Manuel Frage, 110
Israel, 3, 11n, 20, 49, 57, 91, 93
Istanbul, 35, 36, 51
Italy, 11n, 23, 46, 64, 65, 68, 69, 74, 76–84, 114n

Jaffa, 89
Japan, 20
Jasenovaae, 70
Jerusalem, 89
John Paul II, Pope, 70, 71
Jover, José Mariá, 108, 115n
Juan Carlos I, King, 108
Juliá, S., 115n

Kamen, Henry, 110
Khalidi, Walid, 93
Koestler, Arthur, 90
Koletis, Ioannis, 42n
Kontoglou, Fotis, 39
Kordatos, Yannis, 37
Korea, 20
Koselleck, Reinhart, 7

Labanca, N., 83
Lambros, Spyridon, 32, 37
Lavisse, Ernest, 3
Le Goff, J., 75, 76
Lebanon, 88
Levi, Giovanni, 6
Levi, Primo, 84
Lewis, Bernard, 54–5
Liakos, Antonis, 3, 78
Libya, 82
Lisbon, 110
Lowry, Heath, 54

Macedonia, 29
Mack Smith, Dennis, 84
Malta, 81
Mantran, Robert, 54
Marrus, Michael, 5
McCarthy, Justin, 54
Mecadonia, 18, 19
Megas, George, 20

Menéndez y Pelayo, Marcelino, 102, 103
Mercouri, Melina, 15
Michelet, Jules, 3
Middle East, 57, 71
Mohammed, the Prophet, 102
Monod, Gabriel, 1
Montanelli, I., 114n
Moulin, Jean, 11n
Mouradian, Claire, 52
Moustoxidis, Andreas, 36, 42n
Mussolini, Benito, 11n, 74, 82, 95

Nablus, 89
Nice, 81
Nile, 29, 88
Nolte, Ernest, 63, 69, 72n
Nora, Pierre, 75, 79, 99
North Atlantic Treaty Organization, 23, 108
Novotny, Antonin, 63

Olick, Jeffrey, 100
Oslo, 10
Otho, 18
Ottoman Empire, 16, 33, 49, 50, 51, 52, 89

Pacific islands, 95
Palestine, Palestinians, 3, 49, 56, 87–94
Papadopoulos, George, 17–18
Papandreou, Andreas, 15, 16, 39
Paparrigopoulos, Constantinos, 17, 32–3, 34, 35, 37, 38
Papon, Morris, 5
Paris, 40
Parker, Geoffrey, 115n
Pavilae, Ante, 70
Pavone, Claudio, 5
Paxton, Robert, 5
Peloponnesian Wars, 34
Pezzino, P., 81
Philip II, King, 95, 102, 103, 110
Philip of Macedonia, 16, 19
Pikionis, Dimitris, 39
Pinochet, Augusto, 97, 111
Pius XII, Pope, 71, 72
Politis, Nikolaos, 20
Porciani, Ilaria, 79
Portugal, 98–9
Primo de Rivera, Miguel, 101

Quintilian, 75

Rakosi, Matyas, 63
Ranger, Terence, 28
Renan, Ernest, 77
Rethemnos, 19, 20, 23–4
Ricoeur, Paul, 29
Ritsos, Yannis, 39
Rochat, G., 83
Roksandic, Drago, 4
Roman Empire, 2, 32
Romano, Sergio, 62–3, 64, 114n
Rome, 24
Romiti, Cesare, 63–4
Russia, 14, 38, 51, 52

Safed, 89
Sakellariou, Michael, 38
Sanbar, Elias, 3
Sathas, Constantinos, 42
Savoy, 81
Schinas, Constantine, 30
Seferis, George, 27, 28, 39
Serbia, 14, 29
Shaw, Ezel Kural, 54
Shaw, Stanford J., 54
Sicily, 82
Skliros, George, 37
Smyrna, 51
Socrates, 16
Sogno, Edgar, 62, 63
Soviet Union, 15, 57, 71
Spain, 46, 62–3, 64, 65, 95–113
Spanish Civil War, 62–3, 66, 96, 97, 98, 103, 108
Spanish–American War, 95
Spielberg, Steven, 8
St James the Apostle, 102
Stepinaae, Cardinal, 70, 72
Stewart, Charles, 16
Strabo, 2
Suárez, Adolfo, 109
Svoronos, Nikolaos, 35, 38–9, 40
Syria, 88

Talaat, Pasha, 51
Tambiah, Stanley, 14
Theodorakis, Mikis, 39
Thessaloniki, 29
Thompson, Michael, 22
Tilgher, Adriano, 76
Tipaldos, Kozakis, 31
Tobia, Bruno, 79
Torres, Ruiz, 3
Touvier, Paul, 5
Trent, 77
Trieste, 77
Triulzi, Alessandro, 82, 83
Trobriand Islands, 17
Tunisia, 82
Turkey, 19, 49, 56–7, 59
Tusell, J., 100
Tyrrhenian Sea, 82

Ukraine, 71
United Nations, 56
United States, 5, 23, 71, 95

Vakalopoulos, Apostolos, 38
Valencia, 104, 111
Valensi, Lucette, 4
Vatican, 70
Vesga, José Manuel González, 109
Vichy, 2, 5, 66
Victor Emmanuel II, King, 79
Vidal-Naquet, Pierre, 11n
Vives, Jaume Vicens, 115n
Voltaire, François Marie, 32
Vrailas, Petros, 31

Wars of Religion, 2
Warsaw, 85
Woolf, Stuart, 84
World War I, 49–58, 82, 88, 89
World War II, 11n, 38, 54, 63, 83, 95, 97

Yannaras (Giannaras), Christos, 18, 21
Yugoslavia, 4, 48, 70

Zambelios, Spyridon, 17, 31
Zurayk, Constantin, 92